CRYPTOCURRENCY

Cryptocurrency, Blockchain, Ethereum, Bitcoin – The Complete Guide To Understanding FinTech

George Icahn

Introduction 13
Cryptocurrency Secrets + Newsletter. 17
CHAPTER ONE 19
    What is Cryptocurrency? 19
        Ledger Solution 21
    How did Cryptocurrency come about? 26
    What is a cryptocurrency address? 28
    Decentralization and its advantages 29
    The Blockchain network 33
    Summary 37

CHAPTER TWO 39
    Mechanics of Cryptocurrency 39
    Types of Digital Currencies 42
    Limitations and Improvements 50
    Advantages of Digital Currencies 51
    Applications of Cryptocurrency 60
    Storing cryptocurrencies- Digital wallets 73
    Summary 80

CHAPTER THREE 82
    Mining Cryptocurrency 82
    Mining Hardware 87
    How Cryptocurrency will Change the Economy For the Better
    95
    A boost to global remittances 96

Unleashing the potential of e-commerce 97
Faster, cheaper bank transfers 98
Save money for the poor 99
Programmable money and smart contracts 100
Summary 101

Conclusion 102
More Books By George Icahn 103
Introduction 110
Cryptocurrency Secrets + Newsletter 113
Chapter 1: Getting Started With Blockchain 115

What is Blockchain? 115
The History of Blockchain 120
What You Need to Know About Cryptocurrency 125
    What is a Cryptocurrency Address? 126
    Concept of a Digital Wallet 126
    Different Types of Cryptocurrencies 128

Chapter 2: Current World of Blockchain 137

Blockchain Mining and Investment 137
    Blockchain Mining 137
    Blockchain Mining Hardware 139
    Blockchain Mining Software 141
    Mining Difficulty 142

Blockchain Investment 143

Useful Tips From Experts for Cryptocurrency Miners and
Users 146

    Privacy Tips 147

    Proxy Security 148

    Browse on TOR 149

    Virtual Private Network (VPN) 150

    Other Useful Tips 152

Latest News and Information Regarding Blockchain 157

Cryptocurrency Legalities, Taxes, and Regulations 166

    Legal and Regulatory Issues Surrounding Blockchain
    Technology 166

    Defining Blockchain Use 172

    Blockchain Taxation in the USA 172

Chapter 3: Movement of the Future—Blockchain 175

    Revolution of Banking and Marketing 175

        Securing Digital Identity 179

        Rebranding Healthcare 181

        Relevance in Real Estate 185

    Application in Government Structure 189

        4 Ways That Blockchain Technology Can Help Governments
        190

    Blockchain in Governments 191

    Engineering Development in Poorer Countries 193

Chapter 4: Future Use of Blockchain Technology 198
Conclusion 201
More Books By George Icahn 202
About this book 207
Introduction to Ethereum 207
Cryptocurrency Secrets + Newsletter
.... 209
CHAPTER 1 210
 Understanding Ethereum 210
 Ethereum developers and its early days 214
 Early Days 215
 Progress Made So Far 217
 Ethereum's Timeline 224
 The Ethereum Foundation 226

CHAPTER 2 231
 Ethereum as a Cryptocurrency 231
 Transactions 234
 Ethereum's Blockchain 236
 Block Size 237
 Blockchain Size 237
 Block Times 238
 Ethereum's Consensus Algorithm 239
 Why Proof of Stake? 242

What would be the repercussions of the proof of stake on Ethereum price?...244

- Mining Ethereum 246
- The Ethereum Virtual Machine 246
- Solidity.. 247
- Ethereum's Supporting Technologies 249

CHAPTER 3 253

- Trading and Availability....................................... 253
- The "Gas" 257
- A Closer Look at the Market 258
- Pricing.. 258
- Market Movement 259
- Global Adoption 260
- Challenges Facing the Growth 261
- PROFERRED SOLUTIONS 265
- Development Timeline 271
- Latest News On Ethereum 273

Conclusion 283

More Books By George Icahn............ 284

Introduction 291

Cryptocurrency Secrets + Newsletter
.... 296

CHAPTER 1 298

- Who is Satoshi Nakamoto? 298

- What is Cryptocurrency? 300
- How Bitcoin Rose to Fame 306
- Bitcoin Legitimacy and Decentralization 312
    - Bitcoin Legitimacy 312
    - Bitcoin's Decentralized Nature 315
- Summary 319

CHAPTER 2 321

- Bitcoin Creation and Mining 321
    - Bitcoin Creation 321
    - Bitcoin Mining 323
- Bitcoin Mining Hardware 325
- Bitcoin Mining Software 327
- Mining Pools 329
- Mining Difficulty 330
- Bitcoin Wallet 331
    - Paper wallet 333
    - Software wallet 335
    - Mobile Wallet 338
    - Web Wallet 338
- Transferring Bitcoins between Wallets 340
- Buying and Selling Bitcoin (trading) 340
    - Buying Bitcoin 340
    - Selling Bitcoin 344
    - Selling Bitcoin online 344

- Direct trades 345
- Exchange trades 346
- Peer-to-peer trading marketplaces 347
- Identity 347
- Selling Bitcoin offline 348
- Risks of Investing in Bitcoin 348
- Summary 351

CHAPTER 3 352
- Bitcoin Trading Guide 352
  - The Basics 352
  - Tracking with Mobile Apps 353
  - Things to Avoid 356
- Online and Offline Bitcoin spending 359
  - Online spending 359
  - Donating Bitcoin online 360
  - Spending Bitcoin offline 360
- What to do if you have a business of your own 361
- Uses of Bitcoin 369
- Contemplating the prospects of Bitcoin 373
- Summary 375

Conclusion 377
More Books By George Icahn 379

Cryptocurrency

The Complete Guide To Understanding Cryptocurrencies

George Icahn

© **Copyright 2017. All rights reserved.**

No part of this book may be reproduced or transmitted in any form or by any means, electronic or mechanical, including photocopying, recording, or by any information storage or retrieval system without prior written permission from the author or copyright holder except in the case of brief quotations embodied in reviews.

Although the author has exhaustively researched all sources to ensure the accuracy and completeness of the information contained in this book, we assume no responsibility for errors, inaccuracies, omissions, or any inconsistency herein. Any slights of people or organizations are unintentional. Reader should use their own judgment and/or consult a financial professional for specific applications to their individual needs.

Introduction

Cryptocurrency Secrets + Newsletter

CHAPTER ONE

    What is Cryptocurrency?

        Ledger Solution

    How did Cryptocurrency come about?

    What is a cryptocurrency address?

    Decentralization and its advantages

    The Blockchain network

    Summary

CHAPTER TWO

    Mechanics of Cryptocurrency

    Types of Digital Currencies

    Limitations and Improvements

    Advantages of Digital Currencies

    Applications of Cryptocurrency

    Storing cryptocurrencies- Digital wallets

    Summary

CHAPTER THREE

Mining Cryptocurrency

Mining Hardware

How Cryptocurrency will Change the Economy For the Better

A boost to global remittances

Unleashing the potential of e-commerce

Faster, cheaper bank transfers

Save money for the poor

Programmable money and smart contracts

Summary

Conclusion

More Books By George Icahn

Introduction

Cryptocurrency has been described as 21-century money that is fast paced in effectiveness and guarantees prompt action. But there are many misinformed individuals out there with false information on what cryptocurrency really entails. And it is not their fault; there is so much noise and chatter, so much conflicting information about the world of digital currency. Even gurus and pros that are used to investing can easily find their head spinning as they try to get the truth from the sea of lies that are all around us daily we are bombarded with different news about digital currency.

As a matter of fact, at the heart of digital currency is a sense of rebellion against these fees, some of which are so deeply buried in fine print as to be considered "hidden." Along those same lines, the rate of inflation that can potentially diminish the purchasing power of your government-issued legal tender (such as the US dollar) doesn't touch the value of any alternative currency you hold.

Digital currency affords its users complete anonymity. The attraction for cryptocurrency is that it is transparent to governments in its movement and that it is difficult for governments to control access to it. So if you want to buy a large quantity of some illegal substance, you can purchase it from anywhere in the world with Cryptocurrency and no one can tell. Or if you want to bribe a government official, and not have anyone able to tell you did, you could use a cryptocurrency and do your business without alerting anybody.

Some people even look at it as an investment, but while that be profitable, it is a commodity and can go down in value as easily as go up. When you make a purchase with your ATM or credit card, your personal information—your name, physical address and often other identifying data—is attached to each and every transaction. Businesses, banks, and governments can use this data to track you and take note of your purchases. In contrast, cryptocurrency transactions carry no personal information without you adding it yourself.

Accounts that hold traditional currency can be garnished or frozen completely; the latter means the holder of the account has no access to the funds in it. Since cryptocurrency exists outside the regulations and laws that allow this to happen, it's very rare for an investor to be rendered unable to access his coins—though, in certain situations in which illegal activity is proven to have taken place, it can happen.

Cryptocurrencies are fast becoming more popular with each passing day, with the failings of our current financial systems becoming more widespread and the search for better alternatives gaining more campaign. Their advantages over the regular paper money are numerous like the fact that they are not linked directly to the laws and regulations of any government, corporation or bank. The fact that there are no interest rates, fees and other unnecessary charges on petty transactions, as opposed to the current protocols of the financial institutions today is another reason why many are ready to try it out. It is as if people are been cheated on with their own money. To own a credit or debit card, you pay; to transfer funds, you pay. But with cryptocurrencies, such frustrating charges are eliminated. The truth is said, we need a way out.

The purpose of this book is to provide you with the facts and authentic information, the ones you can trust on cryptocurrency. Different aspects of it will be discussed in detail like its origin, its advantages, and the financial and non-financial applications of cryptocurrencies. You will also be taken through the process of creating new cryptocurrencies and how you can trade with it. Valuable comments from experts are included for those who will be excited about this new project but do not know how to go about it. They will find the useful trading tips very interesting. Finally, we will consider the different ways that digital currencies will change the face of our economy for the better in years to come.

You are about to know the truth about cryptocurrencies. Before we get started I would like to offer you exclusive access into my inner circle. This is where we will cover everything cryptocurrency – I promise you'll love it. There is Tons of content and improvements planned (see my offer in the next page).

Cryptocurrency Secrets + Newsletter

Join my **FREE** Cryptocurrency Newsletter to start receiving more information related to everything FinTech. It will help you stay on track, and you will also be notified about my new books (at a special discounted price).

The best part? When you subscribe, you will immediately receive my ***Cryptocurrency Secrets*** report, where you will discover exciting content, such as *The type of cryptocurrencies available, strategies for investing, how to collect more bitcoin, and much more!* It's just my way of saying thank you for your readership!

Follow The Link Below To Subscribe And Get Free Instant Access:

cryptocurrencystudio.com/offer

CHAPTER ONE

What is Cryptocurrency?

Cryptocurrency is a digital type of currency in which encryption techniques are utilized to regulate the generation of units of the currency and verify the transfer of funds, operating independently of a central bank. They are decentralized and provide a platform for personal wealth that is beyond restriction and corruption.

The dictionary defines cryptocurrency as a digital type of currency that is designed to work as a medium of exchange, using cryptography to create the transactions and to facilitate the creation of additional digital currencies. It offers more benefits than the customary paper money that we all are familiar with. Does it sound like magic? Impossible? Well, let me explain the whole concept using an illustration.

You and I are seated on a park bench. It's a great day. I have one orange with me, I hand it over to you, and you now have one orange and I have zero. That was simple, right? Let's look closely at what happened: My orange was physically put into your hand. You know it happened; I was there and you were there. You touched it. We didn't need a third person there to help us make the transfer. We didn't need to pull in Uncle Josh to sit with us on the bench and confirm that the orange went from me to you. The orange is yours and I can't give you another orange because I don't have any left. I can't control it anymore. The orange simply left my possession completely and you have full control over that orange now. You can give it to your friend if you want, and then that friend can give it to his friend. And so on.

So that's what an in-person exchange looks like. I guess it's really the same, whether I'm giving you a banana, a book, or say a quarter, or a dollar bill. Now say, I have one digital orange. Here, I'll give you my digital orange. How do you know that that digital orange that used to be mine, is now yours, and only yours? Think about it for a second. It's more complicated, right? How do you know that I didn't send that orange to Uncle Josh as an email attachment first? Or to your friend Joe? Or to my friend Lisa too?

Maybe I made a couple of copies of that digital orange on my computer. Maybe I put it up on the internet and one million people downloaded it. As you see, this digital exchange is a bit of a problem. Sending digital oranges doesn't look like sending physical oranges. Some brainy computer scientists actually have a name for this problem: it's called the double-spending problem. But don't worry about it. All you need to know is that it's confused them for quite some time and they've never solved it until now. But let's try to think of a solution on our own.

Ledger Solution

Maybe these digital oranges need to be tracked in a ledger. It's basically a book where you track all transactions—an accounting book. This ledger, since it's digital, needs to live in its own world and have someone in charge of it. Blizzard, the guys who created the online game, have a "digital ledger" of all the rare flaming fire swords that exist in their system. So, cool, someone like them could keep track of our digital oranges. Will that not provide the answer?

There's a bit of a problem though: What if some guy single-handedly created more? He could just add a couple of digital oranges to his balance whenever he wants! Another problem is that it is not exactly like when we were on the bench that one day. It was just you and me then. Going through that computer is like pulling in Uncle Josh (a third-party) out of court for all our park bench transactions. How can I just hand over my digital orange to you, like, you know— the usual way?

Is there any way to closely replicate our park bench, just you-and-me, transaction digitally? It seems like it won't be that easy.

So how do you solve this problem? What if we gave this ledger—to everybody? Instead of the ledger living on a single computer, it'll live on everybody's computers. All the transactions that have ever happened, from all time, in digital oranges will be recorded in it. You can't cheat it. I can't send you digital oranges I don't have because then it wouldn't sync up with everybody in the system. It'd be a tough system to beat especially if it got really big. Plus it's not controlled by one person, so I know there's no one that can just decide to give himself more digital oranges. The rules of the system were already defined at the beginning. And the code and rules are open-source—you know, kind of like the software used on your Android phone or kind of like Wikipedia. It's there for the smart people to contribute to, maintain, secure, improve on, and check on. You could participate in this network too and update the ledger and make sure it all checks out. For the trouble, you could get like 25 digital oranges as a reward. In fact, that's the only way to create more digital oranges in the system.

Now let's break it down a little, but that system I explained exists. It's called the cryptocurrency protocol. And those digital oranges are the cryptocurrencies within the system. Fancy!

So, did you see what happened? What exactly does the public ledger enable?

It is an open source remember? The total number of oranges was defined in the public ledger at the beginning. I know the exact amount that exists. Within the system, I know they are limited (scarce).

When I make an exchange I now know that digital orange certifiably left my possession and is now completely yours. I used to not be able to say that about digital things. It will be updated and verified by the public ledger.

Because it's a public ledger, I didn't need Uncle Josh (third-party) to make sure I didn't cheat, or make extra copies for myself, or send the same oranges twice, or thrice...

Within the system, the exchange of a digital apple is now just like the exchange of a physical one. It's now as good as seeing a physical orange leave my hand and drop into your pocket. And just like on the park bench, the exchange involved two people only. You and me—we didn't need any third party there to make it valid.

In other words, it behaves like a physical object.

But you know what's cool? It's still digital and we can now deal with 1,000 oranges, or 1 million oranges, or even 0.0000001 oranges. I can send it with a click of a button, and I can still drop it in your digital pocket if I was in Nigeria and you were all the way in New York City.

I can even make other digital things ride on top of these digital oranges! It's digital after all. Maybe I can attach some text on it — a digital note. Or maybe I can attach more important things; like say a contract, or a stock certificate, or an ID card. So, this is great! How should we treat or value these "digital oranges"? They're quite useful, aren't they?

Well, a lot of people are arguing over it now. There's debate between this and that economic school: between a politician and between programmers. Don't listen to all of them though. Some people are smart. Some others are misinformed. Some say the system is worth a lot, some say it's actually worth zero. Some guy actually put a hard number: $2000 per orange. Some say its digital gold; some say it's a currency. Other say they're just like tulips. Some people say it'll change the world, some say it's just a fad. They may have their own opinion of it though. But by now I think you now know more about cryptocurrency than most of them.

So, when we talk about cryptocurrency we're talking about a purely digitized currency. It is made using cryptography (the study and analysis of secret coding and coding methods), making it nearly impossible to counterfeit, and the way in which cryptocurrency came about is most interesting indeed, because it was and still is a rebellion against the current monetary system that many people see as corrupt, but necessary.

How did Cryptocurrency come about?

It's easy to assume digital currency has been around since the late 1990s; that's about the time the Internet really took off in the public eye, and people started making bill payments and purchases online. So it might be surprising to learn cryptocurrency wasn't even discussed as a concept until 2008. That was when Satoshi Nakamoto outlined the principles and functions of what would be developed and introduced as Bitcoin the following year. The legendary but anonymous Satoshi Nakamoto, a software developer and inventor at the time, published a paper called Bitcoin for a peer to peer payment method. The paper was titled: "Bitcoin- A Peer-to-peer Electronic Cash System. The paper's abstract says that bitcoin is "purely a peer-to-peer version of electronic cash" and it will "allow online payments to be sent directly from one party to another party without going through a financial institution. Digital signatures provide part of the solution but the main benefits are lost if a third party is still required to prevent double spending". He continued by saying "we propose a solution to double spending problem using a peer-to-peer network. The network timestamps transactions by hashing them into an ongoing chain of hash-based proof-of-work, forming a record that cannot be changed without redoing the proof-of-work. The longest chain not only serves as a proof of the sequence of the events witnessed but proves that it came from the largest pool of CPU power. As long as a majority of CPU powers is controlled by nodes that are not cooperating to attack the network, they will generate the longest chain and outpace attackers. The network itself requires minimal structure. Messages are broadcasted on a best effort basis, and nodes can leave and rejoin the network at will, accepting the longest proof-of-work chain as proof of what happened while they were gone".

Although Bitcoin was the first ever official cryptocurrency, the big fish in a small pond for about two years, it was literally the *only* fish. No wonder most people think only of Bitcoin when they hear others talk of digital currencies or cryptocurrencies. They were the first and got all the media attention for the longest time. More players have emerged, of course; since 2011, digital currencies such as Litecoin, Peercoin, Novacoin, and Namecoin—to name just a few—have made their presence known. There are now about 900 different kinds of cryptocurrencies—and that number's likely to grow.

But looking at what cryptocurrency offers, the promise of a cost-effective transaction as opposed to the frivolous fees charged customers both for online and offline deals, as well as its decentralized nature, it doesn't really matter whether or not the true identity of its founder is verified or not. Even though no one knows exactly who he is, his identity is irrelevant and it is only useful for historical records.

What is a cryptocurrency address?

Just like a literal address helps others locate and confirm your ownership of a property, so is the cryptocurrency address. It is unique for every customer. It is a public address that utilizes a number of unique characters to receive cryptocurrencies. It proves your ownership because each of this public address has a matching, corresponding private address linked to it, and this private address is also linked to the digital ledger, the blockchain. It is just like a special mailbox through which you receive currencies instead of emails

Decentralization and its advantages

It is no longer news that the masses are already growing frustrated and losing faith in the traditional paper-money system and the way centralized banks are treating people's lives and hard-earned money. The world's first decentralized digital currency is Bitcoin, and it is linked to no single person or country, it is under no control of any central bank and it cannot be minted on plastic, paper or metal.

The presence of intermediaries is the choke-points where the governments can apply pressure in the current centralized financial systems. Take for instance how the problem of double spending is addressed. They entrust an intermediary to keep a ledger (physical) of balances and they deduct a transaction amount from the payer's account and add it to the payee. Long process, stalling because of the involved third party and unnecessary transaction fees, are all problems this type of solution involves.

But with the decentralized nature, the problem of double spending is solved without any need for an intermediary. There is only ever one payer and payee for any particular deal, which makes it literal digital cash. It does this by a publicly distributed ledger of transactions across a peer-to-peer network. Simply put, there is a digital ledger that records all transactions so that digital currency spent by someone cannot be spent by that same person again. There is no single central authority keeping all the funds as this digital ledger is distributed across all nodes. There is also transparency as opposed to the now common calling for oversight into the actions of Federal Reserve accounts. Cryptocurrency transaction records are public and available to everyone connected.

There is no third party regulating the ledger, no governments, no banks, no organization can claim to be in charge of cryptocurrency regulation. Meaning that if you transfer funds in crypto cash to someone or to your wallet (we will discuss this later in details), no one can touch it, nor can they be affected by whatever economic conditions affecting your banks. It is completely untraceable by any entity as it is literally off their radar. It belongs to you 100 percent and not to anyone else. As a result of cryptocurrency's decentralized nature, people all over the world that witnessed, and possibly were victims of the economic recession of 2008 by losing their money, have begun investing and trading with cryptocurrencies.

There are also cases of government tampering with bank notes. Here are some examples.

- In 2017, the Federal Government of Nigeria **confiscated** hard currencies in Naira, Dollars, Pounds, and Euros, belonging to individuals all in the name of fighting corruption.
- In 2016, Syrian refugees had their wealth **confiscated** by border guards.
- In 2016, Venezuela had 720 percent inflation and Bolivar **lost** about 90 percent of its value.
- In 2013, the Government of Cyprus **seized** up to 40 percent of its citizen's money.
- In 2008, Argentina **nationalized** $30 Billion in private pensions.

True, governments are not the only way people lose money, hyperinflations and seizing of funds are serious threats, but wealth can also be stolen by companies or individuals. It is time to give people more control over their wealth, and cryptocurrencies provide just that. Here are some advantages of letting people have control over their wealth:

1. **It accelerates innovation**- If building a new service or product will make people rich; it is likely that more people will try to produce new things. And with more people giving innovation a shot, competition will rise, and we all know competition always brings out the best in people. There will be quality products in the market because they are guaranteed that no one can tamper with their wealth.
2. **People work harder**- When people are sure that their income is always safe, they will work hard knowing that they can make a better life for themselves and their families. But when wealth can be taken from people any minute and without permission, it dampens both their hardworking spirit and their incentive to work harder.
3. **It attracts the best and the brightest**- When a particular field is a sure way to success, people will try and invest in that field. If people

in a specific geographical location are known to have control over their wealth, it is a natural pulling force to the best investors and the brightest organizations.

So, cryptocurrency can solve virtually all the problems experienced in the financial system today. It is resistant to confiscation, less susceptible to hyperinflation, guarantees transparency, eliminates the need for a third party, doesn't waste valuable time and it grants all users a universal access. With digital currencies, one of the fundamental human rights is the right to control one's wealth.

The Blockchain network

The relationship between blockchain network and cryptocurrencies has been likened to what the internet is to email. Simply put, blockchain network is the technology that cryptocurrency transactions are built on and that simplifies our transactions. It is a numerical or digital (online) ledger that records transactions that are made in cryptocurrencies, sequentially and openly. It is different from the current way of banking, where all transactions are linked to a non-visible, centralized network. But the blockchain technology is a decentralized database of the digital ledger and it is made public for all to see. So, it makes it possible to monitor every transaction into details. It is distributed in that, even in the comfort of your room, you can control all your transaction transparently. Each transaction is viewed as a single block, where subsequent transactions or blocks are added to make a digital, linear, chronological chain known as blockchain. Each time a block is completed, a new block is automatically generated. Each computer connected to this network is called a node. So, when a new transaction is recorded, a copy of the blockchain is sent to each node as they join the network. This decentralized database of the digital ledger is replicated and harmonized through the internet by anyone connected so it renders useless the use of a centralized administrator (like banks). This digital ledger is incorruptible (no centralized information available for alteration or hacking) and it records not only financial dealing but also anything that has value (assets).

This ensures that each node or computer connected to this decentralized network has all information about every transaction from the beginning to the most recently completed transaction. All other forms of transactions need a third party or an intermediary for them to work. Middlemen perform simple tasks like keeping records and authenticating the transaction processes. But with blockchain network, you do not need a third party to conduct business. The money, property, and stocks are displayed on the computer as files. So, recreating such files is a lot easier and you don't need a middleman in the whole process at all.

It allows people to trust each other, thereby extending the borders of the transaction. It is also safe as hacking the system is unfathomable. For example, if someone wants to hack into a single transaction or block, he will not just try to alter that block but also the previous block, and the previous block back to the very genesis of the transaction. And here's the worse news, he will then try to gain access to all the millions of computers connected to that network, which could number into millions. So, the possibility of someone hacking into the system is very low, as opposed to the centralized systems we do have today. There have been cases where banking systems are hacked, identities stolen and bank records cleared. None of these is possible with the blockchain technology.

It will have a very great impact on the next generation. It gives all connected to the network equal access unlike the banks and governments today. The elimination of intermediaries makes it possible to conduct transactions with more frequency and efficiency, contributing to the foreseeable high traffic in the local and international trades. It will give more freedom as well, as many countries spend millions of dollars fighting corruption. But with the blockchain network, protection against exploitation and corruption is guaranteed. Even the high number of people who lack exposure to the global economy will now be more familiar with the payment and financial systems. No doubt, blockchain is the blueprint for all cryptocurrencies. Vitali Buterin, developer of the cryptocurrency called Ethereum, made the following comments about blockchain: "A blockchain is a magic computer that anyone can upload programs to and leave the programs to self-execute, where the current and all previous states of every program are always visible, and which carries a very strong crypto economically secure guarantee that programs running on the chain will continue to execute in exactly the way that the blockchain protocol specifies." For a more in-depth look into Blockchain Technology checkout "Blockchain: The Complete Guide To Understanding Blockchain technology" You can find it here: http://cryptocurrencystudio.com/blockchain

Summary

Where do the ideas for cryptocurrency come from? Why do some technologies thrive while many others die? What does it take for complex technical innovations to be successfully commercialized? This chapter has really helped us understand how and why cryptocurrency innovations have moved to greater heights since it started. The most important benefit, which is its decentralized nature, has also been explained. We have seen that it will only guarantee much financial freedom than the current financial system that now rules the world. But in case you are new to the study of cryptocurrency, or maybe you are thinking of trading and investing in it because of its very bright prospects, then this book is a book you should read carefully. In the next chapter, we will discuss the technicalities of cryptocurrency and the various fields in which it can be applied. To further boost and strengthen your confidence in it, we will also learn about its limitations and the corresponding solutions to each challenge faced. Finally, we will discuss how you can store your cryptocurrency assets.

CHAPTER TWO

Mechanics of Cryptocurrency

In a typical currency, like the British Pounds or the U.S. dollars, transactions are handled either through exchanging cash or via electronic transfers. These electronic transfers are managed by large banks that we trust to keep our money safe and our transactions honest.

To create a cryptocurrency, we first have to take the responsibility of keeping track of transactions away from banks and manage it ourselves. The first step is to create a ledger of everyone's payments to everyone else. This ledger will keep track of who owes money to whom and records everyone's payments to each other.

The next step is to prevent people from cheating by adding transactions that one party much not agree on. One easy way to solve that problem is by requiring both people in the transaction to sign off on the payment. Each participant can add their "digital signature" using public/private key encryption so that everyone knows the transaction is legitimate.

What is a digital signature? A digital signature is supposed to be the digital analog to a handwritten signature on paper. We desire two properties from digital signatures that correspond well to the handwritten signature analogy. Firstly, only you can make your signature, but anyone who sees it can verify that it's valid. Secondly, we want the signature to be tied to a particular document so that the signature cannot be used to indicate your agreement or endorsement of a different document. For handwritten signatures, this latter property is analogous to assuring that somebody can't take your signature and snip it off one document and glue it onto the bottom of another one. And it is worth mentioning that a digital signature has a scheme that serves as its foundation. A digital signature scheme consists of the following three algorithms which are:

1. (sk, pk) := generateKeys(*keysize*) The generateKeys method takes a key size and generates

a key pair. The secret key *sk* is kept privately and used to sign messages. *pk* is the public verification key that you give to everybody. Anyone with this key can verify your signature.

2. sig := sign(*sk* , *message*) The sign method takes a message and a secret key, *sk* , as input and

outputs a signature for *message* under *sk*

3. isValid := verify(*pk* , *message* , *sig*) The verify method takes a message, a signature, and a

public key as input. It returns a boolean value, *isValid* , that will be *true* if *sig* is a valid

signature for *message* under public key *pk* , and *false* otherwise.

We require that the following two properties hold:

- *Valid signatures must verify*

    verify (*pk* , *message* , sign (*sk* , *message*)) == true

- Signatures are *existentially unforgeable*

But there's one last problem: Who owns the ledger? In a traditional currency system, a bank would maintain it, but we're supposed to be building a currency that doesn't need banks. Instead, everyone has their own ledger, and all transactions are made public so everyone updates their ledger at the same time.

In this way, everyone can safely exchange money without worrying about whether the people handling it are trustworthy. Instead of trusting a central bank or a government to validate our transactions, we can simply use cryptography to force everyone to play fair. While cryptocurrencies are still in the early stages, in a few years they might be the preferred way to make payments all over the world.

Types of Digital Currencies

In the year 2008, the very first digital currency was created. But the truth is that creation of a cryptocurrency can occur anytime and with the rate of growth that is now synonymous to cryptocurrency, it is expected to increase in the coming years. Since the creation of the first digital currency, many other types of cryptocurrency have hit the market. As of January of 2015, there were more than 500 different types of cryptocurrencies and that number has quickly risen to over 900 as at mid-2017. As earlier noted, the largest and most successful cryptocurrency in the blockchain network is the bitcoin, but there are several others worth mentioning. In rankings, The Bitcoin is followed closely by Ethereum, Ripple, and Litecoin respectively. Even though presently there are some 900 types of cryptocurrencies, that number is still growing. We cannot mention all the 900 different types we have in this book, but for the sake of brevity, let us discuss the top 10 cryptocurrencies currently trending in the market and how they can benefit you, the aim is to get you better acquainted and subsequently motivate you to think about trading with these easy to use and more efficient digital cash.

1. **Bitcoin**

    The Bitcoin, created by the anonymous scientist, Satoshi Nakamoto in 2008, is one of the pioneers of digital currency and can be used to purchase items over the internet (electronically) and Eve in some cases locally. Now it is interesting to find out that you don't need to understand everything about the technicalities of the Bitcoin before you can start using it as a means of exchange. Just install the bitcoin wallet on your electronic device, maybe a computer or a smartphone. It will automatically generate a bitcoin address for you once this is done, and then you can proceed to perform real transactions, in fact, all types of transactions with it. As your need for more transactions increases, you can generate more Bitcoin addresses for yourself. For an in-depth look in Bitcoin you can check out "Bitcoin: The Complete Guide To Understanding Bitcoin" you can get it here: http://cryptocurrencystudio.com/bitcoin

2. **Ethereum**

This decentralized computing platform will foster trust Eve among strangers. You can

do business with virtually anybody because with the Ethereum, all the terms and conditions are clearly spelled out in a "smart contract", digitally registered on the blockchain network. This smart contract functionality offers the Eretheum Virtual Machine [EVM], a virtual machine that verifies and validates all contracts using a cryptocurrency known as "Ether". The embedded "smart contract" can be used multiple times for different transactions. No wonder its market capitalization as of 2017 is the 2nd on the cryptocurrency table, with the only Bitcoin ahead of it. For an indepth look into Ethereum you can check out "Ethereum: The Complete Guide To Understanding Ethereum" you can get it at: http://cryptocurrencystudio.com/ethereum

3. **Ripple**

   It is also known as the Ripple Transaction Protocol (RTXP), and as expected it is built on an open source, (decentralized) internet protocol and currency known as Ripples (XRP). This Ripple protocol uses an agreed process to facilitate all transactions, be it an exchange, payments, as well as withdrawals. It is easy to understand and use as it offers instant, cost-effective payments, both locally and internationally. It was launched in 2013

4. **Litecoin**

   This digital currency, launched in 2011, is almost identical to the Bitcoin in creation.

Some even argue that its creation was inspired by the bitcoin. The transfer policy was built on an open source protocol as well. It is a peer-to-peer cryptocurrency that was released under the MIT (X11) software license.

5. **Dash (Formally known as Darkcoin)**
   This digital currency was launched by Evan Duffield in 2014 and it is a more secretive form of bitcoin as its formal name, Darkcoin shows. Business dealings are almost untraceable as it provides more added privacy. During its launch, two key features of this cryptocurrency that was emphasized were privacy and speed. It has since lived up to its expectation as "dash" has an ever-growing fan base. Its acceptability has not been questioned either.

6. **Peercoin**
   This one-of-its-kind digital currency was created by two software developers namely, Scott Nadal and Sunny King in 2012. Its most unique feature is its combination of

"proof-of-work" and "proof-of-stake". It was formally known as PPcoin. The "proof-of-work" hashing process used in mining this coin initially became difficult gradually. To make up for this, users were rewarded with coins that used the "proof-of-stake" algorithm. The advantage of this remodeled coin is that it requires little energy to generate blocks or in other words, complete a transaction.

7. **Dogecoin**

This digital currency was launched in 2013 and it uses a technology of scripts as a proof-of-work scheme. The makeup was based on the same protocol used in creating the Bitcoin, although there were some modifications. There is no limit to the production of this digital currency and it is best suited for carrying out smaller transactions because this cryptocurrency deals with coins that are of lesser values individually. The block time is approximately 60 seconds.

8. **Primecoin**

In the summer of 2013, software developer Sunny King developed this digital currency. Its technicality, which is the proof-of-work, was based on prime numbers, totally different from the Bitcoin framework. It works to find unique long chains of prime numbers, thereby providing greater mining ease and added network security.

9. **Chinacoin**

    You probably think it was made in China or the developer is named China, right? No. It was not created in China. It is based on the same framework as with the Litecoin. It uses the script key derivation function, which is password based. It is generated in 60 seconds block, with 88 coins per block. Amazing!

10. **Ven**

    This digital currency was launched in 2007 and it was created to reduce the risk of inflation. Its value in the financial market is determined from a list of currencies, commodities and carbon features.

As the above review of the top 10 in the current market shows, cryptocurrency is not all about Bitcoin. In fact, the well-known Bitcoin has alternatives like the Auroracoin, Mastercoin, Freicoin, Quark, Sexcoin, Namecoin, e.t.c. There is a host of other types of digital currencies to choose from. Based on CoinMarketCap.com, a website that regularly publishes the market capitalization of cryptocurrencies, there are about 20 types of digital currencies

Limitations and Improvements

Many people do point to the fact that cryptocurrencies can only be accessed and harnessed over the internet as one limitation of this new innovation, while some others mention the ignorance of the over 40 percent of the world's population to the existence of digital currencies as the reason why it pegs a little backward in comparison to paper money. But these are really not big issues. Remember the saying: No Pain No Gain! They are just excuses, not challenges. Before we talk about the issues that are obstructing the growth of cryptocurrencies, let us briefly mentions the advantages.

Advantages of Digital Currencies

Freedom in Payment

With digital currencies, it is possible to be able to send and get money anywhere in the world at any given time. You don't have to worry about crossing borders, rescheduling for bank holidays or any other limitations one might think will occur when transferring money. You are in control of your money with cryptocurrencies and there is no central authority figure in the network or a third party needed to make the deal go through.

Control and Security

Allowing users to be in control of their transactions help keep the economy of cryptocurrency safe for the network. Merchants cannot charge extra fees on anything without being noticed. They must talk with the consumer before adding any charges. Payments in crypto cash can be made and finalized without one's personal information being tied to the transactions.

Due to the fact that personal information is kept hidden from prying eyes, cryptocurrency protects against identity theft and the general problem of double spending. Digital currencies can be backed up and encrypted to ensure the safety of your money.

Immediate Settlement

Purchasing real property typically involves a number of third parties (Lawyers, Notary), delays, and payment of fees. In many ways, the Bitcoin/cryptocurrency blockchain is like a "large property rights database," says Gallippi. Bitcoin contracts can be designed and enforced to eliminate or add third party approvals, reference external facts, or be completed at a future date or time for a fraction of the expense and time required to complete traditional asset transfers

Fraud

Cryptocurrencies are digital and cannot be counterfeited or reversed arbitrarily by the sender, as with credit card charge-backs.

Information is Transparent

With the block chain, all finalized transactions are available for everyone to see, however, personal information is hidden. Your public address is what is visible; however, your personal information is not tied to this. Anyone at any time can verify transactions in the cryptocurrency blockchain. A cryptocurrency protocol cannot be manipulated by any person, organization, or government. This is due to digital currencies being cryptographically secure. There are approximately 2.2 billion individuals with access to the Internet or mobile phones who don't currently have access to traditional exchange systems. These individuals are primed for the Cryptocurrency market. Kenya's M-PESA system, a mobile phone-based money transfer, and micro financing service recently announced a Bitcoin (a digital currency) device, with one in three Kenyans now owning a bitcoin wallet.

Very Low Fees

Currently, there are either no fees or very low fees within digital currency payments. With transactions, users might include fees in order to process the transactions faster. The higher the fee, the more priority it gets within the network and the quicker it gets processed. Digital Currency exchanges help merchant process transactions by converting cryptocurrency into fiat currency. These services generally have lower fees than credit cards and PayPal. There aren't usually transaction fees for cryptocurrency exchanges because the miners are compensated by the network. Even though there's no cryptocurrency transaction fee, many expect that most users will engage a third-party service, such as Coinbase, creating and maintaining their own cryptocurrency wallets. These services act like Paypal does for cash or credit card users, providing the online exchange system for digital currency, and as such, they're likely to charge fees. It's interesting to note that Paypal does not accept or transfer crypto cash.

Fewer Risks for Merchants

Due to the fact that cryptocurrency transactions cannot be reversed, do not carry with them personal information, and are secure, merchants are protected from potential losses that might occur from fraud.

With digital cash, merchants are able to do business where crime rates and fraud rates may be high. This is because it is very hard to cheat or con anyone trading in digital currencies due to the public ledger, otherwise known as the blockchain.

Seeming Setbacks or Limitations

Cryptocurrencies have taken the world by storm as evident from their massive growth and the polarity that they have gained. According to a recent report, if you knew about bitcoins seven years ago and the potential they would have in the future, you would be now $10.4 million richer.

Despite the huge potential and impact that cryptocurrency have in the modern financial world, there are a number of challenges that about them that you should know. Let us briefly look at these challenges.

Lack of Awareness & Understanding

The truth is that many people are still unaware of digital currencies. People need to be educated about cryptocurrencies to be able to apply it to their lives. Networking is a must to spread the word on digital currencies. Businesses are accepting digital cash because of the advantages, but the list is relatively small compared to physical currencies.

Companies like TigerDirect and Overstock accepting the digital currency as payment is great. However, if they do not have a knowledgeable staff that understands digital currencies, how will they help customers understand and use them for transactions?

The workers need to be educated on how digital currencies work so that they can help the customers. This will definitely take some time and effort. Otherwise, what is the benefit of such large companies accepting digital cash if its staff doesn't even know what digital currencies are?

Risk and Volatility

Digital currencies have volatility mainly due to the fact that there is a limited amount of coins and the demand for them increases by each passing day. However, it is expected that the volatility will decrease as more time goes on. As more businesses, media, and trading centers begin to accept the digital currency, its price will eventually settle down. Currently, looking at the market shows that the price of cryptocurrencies bounces every day mainly due to current events that are related to digital currencies.

Still Developing

Digital currencies are still at their infancy stage with incomplete features that are in development. To make the digital currency more secure and accessible, new features, tools, and services are currently being developed. Cryptocurrencies have some growth to do before it comes to its full and final potential. This is because they are just starting out, and it needs to work out its problems just like how any currency in its beginning stage would need to.

Battle between Nations for Control

Nations especially the developed countries are currently battling for control of who plays in their financial system. Some of the nations are also not ready to validate cryptocurrencies at the state level and as a result, numerous cases have filed in court to address these matters.

Complex Technical Aspect

The leaders in the cryptocurrency world, as well as analysts, are concerned about the high degree of complexity of the Blockchain and its scalability. As these digital currencies continue to gain traction, there is a risk of the entire system collapsing due to various issues related to scalability such as bandwidth TPS (transactions per second, DDoS attacks, and Blockchain size. A robust system needs to be put in place to prevent such scenarios from occurring to foster the success and sustainability of cryptocurrencies.

Architecture of Consensus

Proof-of-work (PoW) often results in technological and mining centralization. In addition, Proof-of-stake (PoS) give attackers a golden opportunity to maintain parallel block chains without incurring high costs.

It is also vital to mention that some people fear that their security is under threat as the network makes all transactions transparent. Some fear if the security of their keys, especially their private keys will not be jeopardized at some point. Are you thinking about that too? We will treat this issue more extensively under 'Wallets'. As long as you have a good way of remembering or retrieving your passwords and protecting your computer from viruses, you will find out that there is really nothing to worry about.

These challenges pose a great danger to the sustainability of cryptocurrencies across the globe. Other challenges that we need to be aware of as we continue to invest in various cryptocurrencies is the unpredictable increase in digital currency fees and hyper-volatility.

Limited supply results in high rates and the value are directly linked to the demand in the market. It is also important to note that it is not possible to carry out any form of quantitative easing especially when assessing digital coins because the coins are only made available as fast and the processing networks involved are able to resolve blocks. Irrespective of these challenges, a tremendous growth in value of various cryptocurrencies have been recorded thanks to advancement in the systems that are used to monitor it.

Like we pointed out earlier, without some sacrifices, success may be far off. All the big names today started somewhere, and what they do not tell you is a number of times they fell and picked themselves back up. With

Cryptocurrency, you do not need to fear 'falling down' so to speak. As long as you have all the facts and you know what to expect, the sky is not just the limit but your starting point.

Applications of Cryptocurrency

Making basic amenities accessible- A lack of access to basic amenities like health care and insurance in developing countries is due to lack of income. The money required to have access to these amenities is more than what they make. Also, insurers tend to exploit these low-income earners by siphoning them and increasing the money unnecessarily. Cryptocurrency will ensure that these processes will be restricted to an online mode which will reduce the corrupt insurer's impacts. It will also give customers the option of paying in smaller amounts.

Cheap money transfer- One of the biggest pros of Cryptocurrency is that, compared to other electronic payment systems, it has a very low transaction cost. The low transaction fee is not nearly as costly as the fees on money transfers brokered by banks, credit cards, and commercial software like PayPal. The low costs of transactions in digital currency are especially advantageous for immigrants sending remittance to their families in their home countries. This is a huge potential demographic for cryptocurrency simply because the remittance transfer industry is quite large (about $542 billion was transferred globally in remittance flow in 2013). International transfers can be extremely expensive; in fact, according to the World Bank's report on Remission Prices, the global average fee for such payments was 7.72% during the first quarter of 2015. Last year, there was an estimated $442 billion sent from individuals in developed lands to their families back home in poorer countries. We can't question this because they aim to make life better for them. We all will want to help our families in need no doubt. But can you try and imagine the amount of money needed to transfer such a large amount of funds? We all know money is sent by MoneyGram, Western Union money transfer, and other entities like that, and they charge for their services. But using the digitalized digital currencies for such transfers will result in the bypassing of bank charges and the common remittance protocols. More funds will be saved and sent home. Also, such remittances can take significant amounts of time to be verified by the brokering financial institutions. Cryptocurrency like the Bitcoin allows immigrants to send cheap, practically-instant remissions. As of April 2015, the average fee per transaction was 0.000155 BTC (at the time, approximately $0.04 per transaction). The average time between transaction blocks was about 9.11 minutes.

Handling private expenses- One of the biggest advantages of cryptocurrency is its pseudonymous quality (members are identified by the public keys rather than their "real world" identities). For many people, this affords a desired level of privacy that traditional digital payment systems do not. Some examples of situations in which this quality really comes into play include situations in which people are fleeing from abusive partners, desiring controversial health procedures, or operating outside the confines of oppressive governments. Unfortunately, there is also the flip-side of this privacy; capability for cryptocurrency to be used for unethical and criminal purposes. The most infamous example of this is Silk Road – the massive "Deep Web" marketplace. Silk Road used the privacy inherent in cryptocurrency (as well as an anonymous software called TOR) to allow for users to buy and sell contraband. While the moderators of Silk Road didn't allow for the sale of goods resulting from or intended to cause the harm or exploitation of other people, users could still illegally purchase contraband such as illicit drugs and forged identity documents. Digital currencies' relative anonymity could also potentially provide criminals with avenues for money laundering or funding terrorist organizations.

Day to Day purchase- While the above uses are special-interest uses, the average cryptocurrency user will simply use it to normal purchase goods from online (or even physical) retailers. As the cryptocurrency market size grows, this will become increasingly common – the monetary value of cryptocurrency will (theoretically) stabilize, consumers will want to spend their digital cash, and retailers will see the benefits of accepting digital currency transactions. This is a positive development for a few reasons. First, the low transaction costs mentioned above are a great incentive for businesses to accept digital currency payment; merchants can significantly cut their costs by reducing the fees involved in credit card transactions, authorizations, statements, interchanges, and customer service fees. Second, digital currency makes it so the new payment system acts as a stimulus for financial innovation; features, such as micro-payments, which are generally not possible in other financial systems, create new financial opportunities and drive for new online business models and marketing strategies.

Application in Banking- Major Banks (quite a number of them) worldwide are experimenting with the use of digital currencies in other to modernize and simplify banking processes and cut down on costs. Other reasons for wanting to try it out also include the ability to create fresh business models and the high likelihood of competing with fintechs. They are also looking at how digital currencies will help solve some problems they face on a daily basis in their businesses. Banking regulatory entities are also looking to use its framework for developing more efficient regulations. In fact, it will help speed up transactions and make them more secure.

The year 2015 was the year when major financial sectors started thinking about blockchain technology- the power house of all cryptocurrency. It was also stressed that for financial organizations like the Banks to use this technology to their advantage, teamwork, and partnership across the industry is imperative. It was also highlighted that the crypto-cash technology will help to solve some key problems within the financial system. Problems like:

- Prevention of interference to an agreed chain of transactions.
- The issue of double spending
- Problems relating to trust
- Agreement on transaction history

Transparency is another feature of this technology that will benefit both the customers and the banking system. No one will be able to alter any record. In fact, it could save bank's infrastructure by $20 billion a year come 2022.

Transactions today are often verified by a centralized system that keeps its own central ledger. This can slow down transactions as it could take days to settle a deal. It can also take days for two or more banks to relate and agree with a particular customer's records. But the digital currency initiative will eliminate that period of a wait as each bank will have its own copy of the ledger immediately the transactions are lodged. This will enable easy communication among participants. Transactions will be validated in within seconds and significant costs will be cut down.

Marketing will also be transformed. Many marketing procedures today may involve the use of intermediaries, multiple handovers, lengthy processes and the likes. But the application of cryptocurrency will eliminate all these problems. Another thing worth highlighting is that digital currencies allow the use of "smart contracts". This will create a transaction route such that some actions will be approved automatically provided some conditions are met. One example is as long as certain codes are complete, remittances will be approved.

Securing Digital Identity- No matter the field of human endeavor, be it work, business, leisure, politics or healthcare, authorization of identities is directly connected to all of them. But there are challenges facing the concept of identity authorization maybe because of inadequate common comprehension and the mostly unchecked cyberspace of personal information. Technology has advanced in recent times that pose a threat to digital identities like growing cases of hacked databases and account breaches. What cryptocurrency does is using biometrics to provide solutions to these issues concerning digital identity, such that identities can be authorized uniquely in a manner that is unalterable, undeniable and safe.

So how exactly will the digital currencies help secure digital identity? To understand that, we need to first consider how digital identities are represented in the blockchain network (mentioned earlier). When a user's identity is entered into the blockchain network, it is seen as a self-asserted block that contains the user's identity feature. The block also contains the user's private and public keys. Other information that the user's block contains is electricity providers or banks along with their public keys or pins for validation.

The user's relationship with the electrical provider is established by signing in with the public keys.

Gradually other relationships are established between the user and the associated providers, and as more of these relationships are established within the blockchain network, the confidence in the accuracy of the user's identity grows organically. And as more transactions are completed in the name of that user, the 'reputation capital' of that user's identity grows consistently.

In case one or more relationships between the user and the entities change, the difference is noted within the blockchain as a separate block with a unique cryptographically signed timestamp. This creates a cryptographically secured sequence that allows the new verifier to reconcile both previous and current relationships.

Application in real estate- The blockchain technology that powers all cryptocurrencies will allow individuals or organizations transfer information, money or another type of assets quickly and without a need for intermediaries. They can also be used to transfer value with ease as regards Real Estate. We will now examine three different ways the use of cryptocurrency will improve or totally transform real estate for the better.

- Smart Contracts.
- Disintermediation
- Prevention of Fraud

Now let us discuss this one after the other.

Smart Contracts: It seems like one of the best features of the digital currency is the smart contract as it has been seen to be useful in various fields. With it, there will no longer be the case of a party fulfilling its obligations while the other party refuses. It is automated as the contract will go on as long as certain mutually agreed conditions are met. An example is you will get paid as soon as you reach a certain number of the consumer base. There will be fewer court cases as transparency will make frauds a thing of the past.

Disintermediation: Real estate transactions can be complicated at times due to the presence of and need for third parties or intermediaries to make the deals fall through. These third parties may include escrow companies, stock brokers, inspectors, appraisers or even government agencies in some cases. These transactions will be stalled for many days till the intermediaries complete their tasks and it can cost money and waste valuable time. It is like we depend on them for the deals to come to a completion. Why are middlemen needed in transactions related to real estate? Why do we need them to validate our title deeds and other documents? It is because they have skills and licenses that we don't have and they have access to some information that we do not have access to, and these licenses and information are needed for these transactions to fall through. As we already know of the blockchain technology, it is a digital ledger that is made public, access to everyone connected is granted at the same time, without needing any form of permission or without any information being withheld. It means every property will be able to handle transactions themselves anytime without the need for any third party.

Let us take TITLE as an example; the title to a property is just a piece of paper currently. The paper needs to be filled out correctly, signed with possibly a pen, and the middle man, a notary most likely puts a rubber stamp on it. It then goes to the county's recorder who manually puts it in their database. Taking a look at the whole process, you will notice the time that will be wasted as well as money that will be spent to get it into the database. But here is how the use of digital currency can help out and make the processes much simpler. It will replace a paper title; a cryptocurrency (e.g. Bitcoin) will be used to create a digital title. It can then be transferred easily over the internet to the necessary agencies, nullifying the need for a third party and saving valuable time as well.

Prevention of Frauds: In the world of transactions, fraud is a major problem. Everybody wants to make quick money, and so they try all sorts of means ranging from forging different kinds of data and paperwork to misrepresentation of bank invoices and statements, deeds, drivers licenses, all in a bid to help them make more money. Real estate fraud is also common and the rate at which this crime is increasing in recent times is alarming. Even the world's largest and most secure banks still fall victim to such criminal acts once in a while. But how can blockchain technology prevent these criminal acts in real estate? This is what Don Oparah, the C.E.O of London-based IT firm, has to say about how blockchain will improve real estate transactions: "By offering a 100 percent incorruptible resource, whereby a sender and recipient of funds was logged, and where digital ownership of certificates for properties are saved, the blockchain could effectively make forged ownership of documents and false listings a thing of the past. The unique digital ownership of certificates would be almost impossible to replicate and would be directly linked to one property in the system, making selling or advertising properties you do not own impossible. So it is clear that frauds in real estate transactions will be reduced to its barest minimum by blockchain technology.

Helping Small Businesses: It can be very hard for some businesses in these developing lands to apply for a loan and get it approved. This is because, in these countries, access to loans depends majorly on middlemen. Not only has that, these loans, as hard as it is to get also attracts very high-interest rates. Banks also refuse to grant loans in areas well known for corruption and fraudulent acts. But the digital currency innovation will help to nullify the role of these middlemen; will promote transparency which will reduce fraudulent activities. This way, small businesses will get loans and extend their borders.

Providing Relief: Sometimes, non-governmental organizations and foreign companies in richer countries do send money, clothes, and other relief materials to these poorer countries, especially when disaster strikes. In some cases, it turns out that this humanitarian assistance is not used for their intended purposes due to corruption and mismanagement. There is also the challenge of the cost of transporting these relief materials to these target countries. The use of cryptocurrencies for such selfless donations can help in two major ways; it can reduce the cost of transporting them, and will keep track of how these humanitarian aids are used. Donors can actually be confident that what they want to be done with their resources are respected and adhered to.

Storing cryptocurrencies- Digital wallets

If you are already thinking of plunging into the crypto market, I will say congratulations! The next thing you'll want to consider is where you're going to keep all those shiny electronic coins. There are several ways you can store and maintain your cryptocurrency accounts; aptly enough, the programs designed to help you do that are called wallets. As a matter of fact, it's very difficult to have a cryptocurrency account without a wallet associated with it.

The regular wallet you carry—besides being a place to keep family pictures, ticket stubs and whatever else may collect there—is a storage place for your financial tools. Most people keep their bank cards, credit cards and regular bill-and-coin currency in their wallets. Well, a cryptocurrency wallet isn't all that different. They're made to store all the information that's pertinent to your digital currency account, and they come in four different types:

Software Wallets. These are programs—ranging from bare-bones simplicity to very large and complex applications—that are installed on a desktop or laptop computer for account access and maintenance. Since space is less of an issue than it is with mobile wallets (please see below), software wallets sometimes come with added features such as market graphs and mining software, as well. Let us now explore some software wallets that are recommended for easy use.

- **Bitcoin-Qt:** This is the original Bitcoin client and it is suitable for storing only Bitcoin (a type of digital currency). It has the highest security and privacy and stability of any software wallet. The only turn off is that it has fewer feature and it takes up so much space on your computer.
- **Armory:** Armory is an advanced Bitcoin client and as the name suggested, it is software that offers protection. It has expanded features for power users. It offers backup features as well as encryption techniques, including cold storage on offline computers.
- **Multibit:** It is like bitcoin-Qt but it is lighter. Its focus is in being fast and easy to use. It synchronizes with Bitcoin network and in a matter of minutes, it is up and running. It supports a variety of languages and is a perfect choice for people with little interest in technology.
- **Electrum:** This rare software wallet is all about speed and simplicity. It does not use up much of your computer resources or space and that is why many choose it. It uses remote

servers that handle most of the complicated parts of any cryptocurrency system.

In relation to software wallets, the following 2 security measures can help you protect your money.

1. **Encrypt your wallet-** This will make it safe from hackers and viruses. Anytime access to this wallet is required, a password needs to be imputed to decrypt this wallet before any transaction can be done. This will also protect the file on which your private key is stored, the "wallet.dat" file. Although it is still not 100 percent safe because some strong software like the keylogs can be used to crack your password codes. That is why experts recommend that you should own different types of Bitcoin wallets. They also discourage putting large sums of bitcoins in a single wallet. You can put a large sum in your paper wallet and keep some in your software wallet.
2. **Back up your wallet-** This measure is good just in case your computer crashes. We all like backing up our files because we are not sure just when our computer misbehaves. If we can

do that with files, how much more our Bitcoin wallet that holds our money. There are different ways of backing up our wallet. We can use external hard drives, while some have opted for online cloud backups. Just remember that with any online backup comes the risk of hacking

Mobile Wallets. These are smartphone and tablet-friendly apps you can take with you anywhere. These are ideal for investors who like to make purchases on the go. Due to space limitations that are inherent with mobile devices, these tend to be smaller and simpler programs than software wallets.

Web Wallets. Currency exchanges issue this type of wallet, which runs on cloud computing—that means they can be accessed from any computing device, anywhere. Web wallets can come with a trade-off: they're simpler to access, but the online availability of digital currency information can lead to hacking and theft.

Paper Wallets or Cold storage. The codes for your currency can be printed out, and these hard copies can be stored in a regular wallet, just like traditional bill-and-coin currency. These are ideal for traders who intend to invest most of their cryptocurrency, and not use it as much for purchases. Paper wallets—properly stored under lock and key, of course—also give investors a very high level of security in comparison to their digital cousins.

There is also what is known as "hybrid" wallets, which combine the local storage capabilities of software wallets with the universal accessibility of web wallets. Most people in the digital currency field consider these to be enhanced software wallets since they involve the installation of a program on a computing device—and thus most hybrid wallets are categorized as such.

Having taken a closer look not only at the types of wallets there are available to investors but also at some advice about what you should keep in mind when you're shopping around for a wallet, it is important to note that you can transfer your cryptocurrency funds from one wallet to another wallet without stress. For example, many types of currency—and also many exchanges—offer their preferred wallets upon sign-up or initial investment. Only in rare cases are you required to go with the wallet offered in these cases; most of the time, you're free to shop around elsewhere to find one that more closely fits your specific needs.

With that in mind, whether you just want storage for your account, or all the bells and whistles, there's a wallet out there just right for you. Many wallet features deal with security, so we'll also pass along some tips to consider when it comes to keeping your cryptocurrency investment safe. As you'll know, hacked wallets can mean a total loss, so security is critical for your investment.

There's a broad range of choices investors have in the storage and maintenance of their digital currency accounts. As an aid, this section has not only help you to understand the concept of cryptocurrency wallet but what traders should look for in order to find one in line with their purchasing and investing plans. For all intents and purposes, your wallet is your alternative currency account; for the latter to function in any meaningful way, it needs the former. So, you can store your cryptocurrency for future use without any worries about losing your income.

For now, there are few web wallets that provide enough insurance to be used to store value like a bank. One advantage of the web wallet is that you can use your cryptocurrency anywhere with fewer efforts to protect your wallets. But there are good prospects regarding web wallets with its high likelihood of getting more and more secure over time.

How you decide to store your digital currency is really up to how you intend to spend them. If you are thinking to invest long term, then it will be advisable to store a bulk of your digital currency in cold storage or paper wallet. If you are looking to make a simple and short term investment, then the software wallet is your best option. If you are looking to make quick digital currency exchanges, then the web wallet and mobile wallet is what you need.

Summary

If someone is going to convince me to try out a new dish, he or she better tell me what I will enjoy in it in order to stir my emotions in that direction. That is what this chapter has endeavored to do. Talking about what makes cryptocurrency different and how they work (Mechanics), and the different types of it currently making waves in the market. We have also seen the various ways the use of digital cash can be beneficial to humans generally, not just in the future but also in our day-to-day activities. A discussion of the challenges inhibiting its growth as well as a comparison with it advantages has been helpful as well. Finally, the concept of digital wallets and the tips for storing digital cash was touched. In the next chapter, we will look at the process of creating new cryptocurrency and how this initiative will change the face of the global economy.

CHAPTER THREE

Mining Cryptocurrency

Simply stated, this is the process of creating new digital currencies. In terms of the blockchain, it is the process of adding new blocks transactions to the already existing blocks or transactions. Do you want to get into cryptocurrency mining? If you do, we're not going to completely discourage you, but beware that mining digital currency bears some similarities to gold rushes. Historical gold rushes are full of stories of young people rushing off to find fortune and inevitably many of them lose everything they have. A few strike it rich, but even those that do generally endure lots of hardship along the way. But why mining cryptocurrency does share many of the same challenges and risks as traditional gold rushes? We'll see but first, let's look at the technical details. To be a miner, you have to join the mining network and connect to other nodes or computers. Once you're connected, there are six tasks to perform:

1. Listen for transactions. First, you listen for transactions on the network and validate them by checking that signatures are correct and that the outputs being spent haven't been spent before.

2. Maintain block chain and listen for new blocks. You must maintain the block chain. You start by asking other nodes to give you all of the historical blocks that are already part of the blockchain before you joined the network. You then listen for new blocks that are being broadcast to the network. You must validate each block that you receive — by validating each transaction in the block and checking that the block contains a valid nonce (an arbitrary number that could only be used once).

3. Assemble a candidate block. Once you have an up-to-date copy of the block chain, you can begin building your own blocks. To do this, you group transactions that you heard about into a new block that extends the latest block you know about. You must make sure that each transaction included in your block is valid.

4. Find a nonce that makes your block valid. This step requires the most work and it's where all the real difficulty happens for miners.

5. Hope your block is accepted. Even if you find a block, there's no guarantee that your block will become part of the consensus chain. There's bit of luck here; you have to hope that other miners accept your block and start mining on top of it, instead of some competitor's block.

6. Profit. If all other miners do accept your block, then you profit! If any of the transactions in the block contained transaction fees, the miner collects those too. So far transaction fees have been a modest source of additional income, only about 1% of block rewards.

We can classify the steps that a miner must take into two categories.

Some tasks — validating transactions and blocks — help the network and are fundamental to its existence. These tasks are the reason that the cryptocurrency protocol requires miners in the first place.

Other tasks — the race to find blocks and profit —- aren't necessary for the network itself but are intended to incentivize miners to perform the essential steps. Of course, both of these are necessary for digital cash to function as a currency, since miners need an incentive to perform the critical steps.

Basically, there are two main hash-based structures.

1. There's the blockchain where each block header points to the previous block header in the chain,
2. Then within each block, there's a Merkle tree of all of the transactions included in that block.

The first thing that you do as a miner is to compile a set of valid transactions that you have from your pending transaction pool into a Merkle tree. Of course, you may choose how many transactions to include up to the limit on the total size of the block. You then create a block with a header that points to the previous block. In the block header, there's always a 32-bit nonce field, and you keep trying different nonces looking for one that causes the block's hash to be under the target — roughly, to begin with, the required number of zeros. A miner may begin with a nonce of 0 and successively increase it by one in search of a nonce that makes the block valid.

We remember that these blocks make up a chain of transactions or blocks in that digital ledger known as the blockchain. Once these records are recorded, the blockchain makes it public to other connected networks or nodes of the completed block. The node connected to the blockchain network makes use of this information in differentiating between legitimate and illegal Bitcoin transactions or from attempts to re-spend coins that have already been spent. Since the Bitcoin uses the "proof-of-work" function, each transaction or block must contain this hash cash "proof-of-work" in order for it to be considered authentic and acceptable. When the blockchain receives a new block, each node connected to the blockchain tries to verify this blocks' "proof-of-work", then on completion of this verification, validates the block or transaction. It only takes about few seconds to complete all these processes. Upon validation, the new block is added. In this way, the number of blocks added each day is kept in check and remains steady. It is resource-intensive and was specifically designed for this purpose. It allows each blockchain connected node to keep transactions secure and reaching a tamper-resistant agreement.

But mining is also used to introduce new digital currency into the system. When new coins are created, miners are rewarded with the transaction fees. These new coins are distributed in a decentralized manner and it builds confidence in the security of the entire system. Miners also assist in keeping the network secure by a consensus approval of transactions. Mining ensures fairness while keeping the network safe, secure and stable.

We recall that it is a digital, decentralized currency and as such does not need a central government calling the shots or giving the go-ahead to print it and circulate it. Miners use specialized software programs and specially designed mining hardware to create or mine these currencies. They use the software programs to solve arithmetic problems and in exchange for this, are issued a set number of digital currencies. It is a smart way to get the currencies and also encouraging to others that are interested in mining these digital currencies. Let us discuss briefly the components needed to create new digital currency.

Mining Hardware

The hardware for mining digital currency is designed to generate the "proof-of-work". There is much hardware to choose from, but your choice of hardware will be determined by a number of factors including the type of coin you want, hashing algorithm and the general acceptability of the hardware, in terms of user's ratings. What exactly is the above-mentioned hashing algorithm or hashrate? It is the rate that controls how many attempts a miner makes in solving a block per second. The more attempts at solving a crypto block, the greater the chances of solving the block and the better the mining hardware. The hashrate is measured in hash per second (H/s). We can have Kilohash (KH/s), Megahash (MH/s), Gigahash (GH/s), Tetrahash (TH/s), and the Petahash (PH/s). Below is a table that discussed the top three cryptocurrency hardware in details.

Hardware name	Avalon 6	AntMiner S7	AntMiner S9
Hashrate	3.5 TH/s	4.73 TH/s	11.8 TH/s
Power usage	1050 watts	1350 watts	1350 watts
Power efficiency	0.29 Joules per GH	0.28 Joules per GH	0.1 Joules per GH
Controller	Separate	Built-in	Built-in

Noise	55 dB	62 dB	50 dB
Chip process	28 nm	28 nm	16 nm
Breakeven point	7 years	2.6 Years	0.9 Years

Of course, there is much hardware to choose from. If you think of mining, the above ones are most recommended.

Mining Software

The major work of creating a digital currency is done by the mining hardware, but the mining software is also playing an indispensable role. It is needed to link the mining hardware to the blockchain network (we discussed that earlier). Just like with the hardware, a number of factors must be considered in choosing which software program will be useful for you in your cryptocurrency mining process. These factors include the operating system and the type of cryptocurrency you plan to create. One thing to take note of is that there are upwards of 900 different types of digital currencies as of 2017 and each of these digital currencies has specialized software for them. That means if you are planning on creating Bitcoin, for example, the software used in the creation of Dogecoin may not work for you. Although it must be noted that, some software can be used to create more than one type of cryptocurrency. Mining software is fairly straightforward – is the software you need to install on your rig that works to solve the cryptographic hashes. There are many digital currency mining apps out there including the following:

- ZOTAC 750 T 1GB (5.35 MH/s for Lyra 2v2)
- 50Miner – A GUI frontend for Windows(Poclbm, Phoenix, DiabloMiner)
- BFGMiner – Modular FPGA/GPU miner in C
- BTCMiner – Bitcoin Miner for ZTEX FPGA Boards
- Bit Moose – Run Miners as a Windows Service.
- Poclbm – Python/OpenCL GPU miner (GUI (Windows & client version of Poclbm (GUI)

- DiabloMiner – Java/OpenCL GPU miner (MAC OS X GUI)
- RPC Miner – remote RPC miner (MAC OS X GUI)
- Phoenix miner – miner
- Cpu Miner – miner
- Ufasoft miner – miner
- Pyminer – Python miner, reference implementation MacOS X))
- Remote miner – mining pool software
- Open source FPGA Bitcoin Miner- a miner that makes use of an FPGA Board
- Flash Player Bitcoin Miner – A proof of concept Adobe Flash Player miner
- XFX 7990 (21.8 MH/s for x11)
- XFX 7990 (28 MH/S for Quark)
- XFX R9 290x black edition (32 MH/s for Ethash)

Mining Pools

The last lesson in mining digital currency is that you should always join a pool of other miners unless you have a ridiculously powerful mining operation and if that's the case you wouldn't be reading this book. Mining pools make it easier to get cryptocurrency more consistently. Essentially, it's a bunch of miners pooling their resources, and sharing the spoils. Historically, when small business people face a lot of risks, they usually form mutual insurance companies to lower that risk. Farmers, for example, would get together and agree that if any individual farmer's barn burned down the others would share their profits with that farmer. Could we have a mutual insurance model that works for small cryptocurrency miners? A mining pool is exactly that — mutual insurance for digital currency miners. A group of miners will form a pool and all attempt to mine a block with a designated coinbase recipient. That recipient is called the pool manager. So, no matter who actually finds the block, the pool manager will receive the rewards. The pool manager will take that revenue and distribute it to all the participants in the pool based on how much work each participant actually performed. Of course, the pool manager will also probably take some kind of cut for their service of managing the pool. Assuming everybody trusts the pool manager, this works great for lowering miners' variance. But how does a pool manager know how much work each member of the pool is actually performing? How can the pool manager divide the revenue commensurate with the amount of work each miner is doing? Obviously, the pool manager doesn't want to just take everyone's word for it because people might claim that they've done more than they actually did.

Mining pools offer shares – a hash is easier to create a pool than solo, and it still provides proof that you have done valid work toward finding the next block. The more shares you can calculate and submit the more fractional ownership you achieve in the next block reward (digital cash reward). Mining pools provide websites with stats and account management, which makes it easy to connect and monitor your hashing power and cryptocurrency unit generation. There are many mining pools out there available for you to join, and unfortunately, we can't tout any one over another within this book. However, a simple Google search for digital currency mining pools will get you started.

Mining Difficulty

Simply stated, this is a measure of difficulty in finding a new block or how difficult it is to find a hash below a given target. The measure is periodically adjusted based on the hashing power that has been deployed by connected miners. There is a global block difficulty, so blocks that are considered valid must hash below this target. The difficulty is adjusted every 2016 blocks, based on the time taken to find the previous 2016 blocks. If one block is discovered every 10 minutes, it will take 2 weeks to find 2016 blocks. If the previous 2016 blocks took longer than 2 weeks to find, the difficulty is reduced. Conversely, if it took less than 2 weeks to find 2016 blocks, as expected the difficulty is increased.

Professional mining- Today mining has mostly moved away from individuals and toward professional mining centers. Exact details about how these centers operate are not very well known because companies want to protect their setups to maintain a competitive advantage. Presumably, these operations maintain profitability by buying slightly newer and more efficient ASICs (Mining hardware) than are available for general sale at a bulk discount. When determining where to set up a mining center, the three biggest considerations are:

- Climate,
- Cost of electricity, and
- Network speed.

In particular, you want a cold climate to keep cooling costs low. Cooling is particularly challenging with cryptocurrency mining, which is estimated to use an order of magnitude more electricity per square foot than traditional data centers (and hence give off an order of magnitude more heat). You obviously want cheap electricity. You also want a fast network connection to be well connected to other nodes in the cryptocurrency peer-to-peer network so that you can hear about new blocks as quickly as possible after they've been announced. Georgia and Iceland have reportedly been popular destinations for digital currency mining data centers.

How Cryptocurrency will Change the Economy For the Better

Looking at digital money, you see a revolutionary technology that allows people or institutions to transfer funds instantly, securely and without a middleman. Digital money can potentially expand international commerce, support financial inclusion, and transform how we shop, save and do business in ways we probably cannot even yet fully understand. From programmable money to new forms of e-commerce, here are five ways the new technology will change the world:

A boost to global remittances

Every year, migrants from developing countries send home more than $500 billion in remittances, a sum that exceeds foreign direct investment. With total fees for international transfers averaging 6-10% for sending $200, the burden on some of the world's most vulnerable people is substantial. Technology has the potential to help these transfers become fast and cheap. Using virtual currency, private users could even send money directly to their families via mobile phone, with the only remaining fees being those charged by the currency exchanges. While traditional money transfer companies have to carry capital to compensate for delays in international money movement, capital requirements are much lower for firms using digital currencies. Of course, capital carrying costs and the cost of money movement comprise only part of the cost for remittance businesses. Nonetheless, reducing these costs might make it easier for smaller players to enter and establish new remittance corridors or for existing players to serve smaller towns or new countries.

Unleashing the potential of e-commerce

Today, concerns over credit card fraud are forcing many online merchants to turn away good business. Such fraud is more common in global transactions, and so many firms do not accept international payments. With a digital currency such as Bitcoin, the transfer cannot be undone once it has been made. This eliminates the risk of fraud for merchants and thus allows them to sell worldwide. And since virtual currencies let customers send funds as easily as email, online shopping would turn into a much smoother process. Digital currency could also allow small businesses in developing countries to engage more in global e-commerce. Latin American vendors could sell hand-crafted goods globally, Chinese teenagers could offer Mandarin tutoring over Skype, and African firms wanting to market their products through online advertising marketplaces would have a payment option that is unavailable today. Small value transactions are a particularly salient use case, as low transaction fees could enable low-value in-app purchases or micro-payments for reading online news articles from media outlets around the globe

Faster, cheaper bank transfers

The way banks move money today is archaic. International bank transfers can take up to a week, with correspondent banks and country-specific clearing houses involved at both ends. Even the cross-border sharing of payment data faces challenges and frictions. By using a digital currency such as Bitcoin, bank transfers could be made instantly, cheaply and safely. In fact, such transfers could even happen without using new currencies. Ripple Labs, for which I am an adviser, supports a protocol that allows clients to transfer funds from one currency to another (say, dollars to euros) using a secure digital ledger. Their technology moves money around the globe in seconds by first finding the most efficient path between trading partners, where the path might consist of a series of transactions among foreign exchange traders who have accounts in a variety of banks, and then confirming all required transactions simultaneously.

Save money for the poor

The explosion of mobile technology in Africa has already shown that developing countries can lead when it comes to sophisticated technology. Estimates suggest that 60% or more of commerce in Kenya takes place using mobile phone credits as a medium of exchange. Anyone with a mobile phone can store money there, and send credits to another user. The problem is that the fees are large: cashing out has historically cost as much as 20%, although the widespread acceptance of the credits means that many consumers are able to spend the credits directly without incurring large fees. Digital currencies could become another convenient and safe form of payment in countries where most citizens don't have bank accounts. While using a digital currency as a second currency in a country would expose citizens there to a certain amount of currency risk, it might be better than the existing options, particularly in high-inflation countries. For example, it would be physically safer than storing cash at home or buying gold jewelry. In addition, someone holding a digital currency could exchange it for a more stable currency on one of the global cryptocurrency exchanges. In this way, it could expand access to international financial markets, allowing even the unbanked a way to save and protect against inflation. One implication may be that capital controls become harder to enforce.

Programmable money and smart contracts

Once an asset is purely digital, it can be moved in automated ways. This paves the way for "programmable money" and "smart contracts". One practical example would be escrow accounts. Such accounts are already used in large transactions, such as property deals. The buyer puts money into escrow, and it only goes to the seller when he or she hands over the title to the property. In the digital age, where the issue of trust can be a key impediment for individuals wishing to transact at arm's length, this system could be used for much smaller sums. Another example is multisig, where money can only be disbursed from an account when multiple individuals authenticate. This could be used to prevent the theft of digital funds, but it could also help firms ensure that money is not "lost" or stolen when it moves across borders, between divisions of a firm, or among charitable organizations and contractors in developing countries.

Programmable money could also have a role in much more complex contracts, such as financial contracts involving multiple parties and complex derivatives. You might put some money in a financial contract which will pay out according to what happens to certain stock prices. A computer program could be linked to stock prices from the Bloomberg terminal feed and then, depending on what happens to certain stocks or certain combinations of stocks, different individuals receive funds.

Summary

This chapter is all about learning the process of mining cryptocurrency and stabilizing the market. We have seen the various components needed for a successful possession of digital currency. We have also seen that a world of digital currency will be a better world as it guarantees much financial freedom and a global financial stability- something the world is yearning for.

Conclusion

There is a fascinating world of various digital currency out there that majority have yet to explore; and for those who have started exploring it, it is not just about the underlying technology alone that brings the excitement but its commercial, social and even commercial possibilities that tickle their fancy. We that are into cryptocurrency already are really amazed at its ability to displace already established institutions, and we believe that eventually, people will find other useful things to do with digital currency, not just commercially but socially as well. Even if your interest is primarily commercial, you'd do well to master the underlying technology — understanding its power and limitations will help you better weather the market's hype cycles. One of the best things about decentralization is that it's a great platform for experimentation and learning. This is your chance to be part of the fastest growing innovation this world has ever seen and if you do, you will be glad you did.

More Books By George Icahn

Check out my Author Central Page:

http://www.cryptocurrencystudio.com/george icahn

BLOCKCHAIN

The Complete Guide To Understanding Blockchain Technology

George Icahn

© **Copyright 2017. All rights reserved.**

No part of this book may be reproduced or transmitted in any form or by any means, electronic or mechanical, including photocopying, recording, or by any information storage or retrieval system without prior written permission from the author or copyright holder except in the case of brief quotations embodied in reviews.

Although the author has exhaustively researched all sources to ensure the accuracy and completeness of the information contained in this book, we assume no responsibility for errors, inaccuracies, omissions, or any inconsistency herein. Any slights of people or organizations are unintentional. Reader should use their own judgment and/or consult a financial professional for specific applications to their individual needs.

Table of Contents

Introduction 110
Cryptocurrency Secrets + Newsletter 113
Chapter 1: Getting Started With Blockchain 115
    What is Blockchain? 115
    The History of Blockchain 120
    What You Need to Know About Cryptocurrency . 125
        What is a Cryptocurrency Address? 126
        Concept of a Digital Wallet 126
        Different Types of Cryptocurrencies 128
Chapter 2: Current World of Blockchain 137
    Blockchain Mining and Investment 137
        Blockchain Mining 137
        Blockchain Mining Hardware 139
        Blockchain Mining Software 141
        Mining Difficulty 142
        Blockchain Investment 143
    Useful Tips From Experts for Cryptocurrency
    Miners and Users 146
        Privacy Tips 147
        Proxy Security 148
        Browse on TOR 149
        Virtual Private Network (VPN) 150

Other Useful Tips... 152
Latest News and Information Regarding Blockchain
.... 157
Cryptocurrency Legalities, Taxes, and Regulations
.... 166
   Legal and Regulatory Issues Surrounding
   Blockchain Technology 166
   Defining Blockchain Use................................... 172
   Blockchain Taxation in the USA 172

**Chapter 3: Movement of the Future—
Blockchain 175**
Revolution of Banking and Marketing 175
   Securing Digital Identity.................................. 179
   Rebranding Healthcare..................................... 181
   Relevance in Real Estate................................... 185
Application in Government Structure 189
   4 Ways That Blockchain Technology Can Help
   Governments 190
   Blockchain in Governments 191
   Engineering Development in Poorer Countries... 193

**Chapter 4: Future Use of Blockchain
Technology 198**
Conclusion... 201
More Books By George Icahn 103

Introduction

Transactions have had a long history dating back to biblical times. At first, they were nonfinancial, as money wasn't in circulation at the time. A credit system was employed where people could conduct transactions and exchange goods and services for a corresponding compensation that was expected immediately or in the future. This method of transaction was disadvantageous, however, as it required one party to absolutely trust the other party to keep their end of the bargain, especially in cases where future recompense was expected. As humans, trust is sometimes a challenge. Then came the common use of trade by barter, where debts were settled by a total exchange of something of corresponding value, such as precious stones, e.g., gold, silver, or diamonds. With the arrival of civilization, coins and other forms of money were introduced, allowing an individual to amass assets. These assets would not deteriorate with time, which was a disadvantage of accumulating goods. This newly introduced form of transaction and amassing wealth had the strong backing of the government or a regulatory body, which was responsible for setting values, adjusting these values, and then regulating circulation.

In the twentieth century, floating currencies gradually replaced the once common fixed currencies, making transactions easier, faster, and less stressful. Even the most complex transactions became easier, but even these transactions still depended on people for various protocols, such as verification, keeping records, and other functions. Tracking documentation, asset authentication, and other back-end functions were occasionally stalled since this transaction system still depended on people to function properly. Computers eventually made transactions easy, but the challenge of cyber theft was always present.

What if a better transaction system could be developed? What if a system could keep track of all transactions without the worry that some transaction records might go missing? What if the records could last forever? What if this transaction system could be applicable for all phases of human society? This book will enlighten you about blockchain technology. Take note of how the current transaction system is improved. Consider how it has been used, although by a minority of the earth's population, and how we all can harness it. Pay attention to its application in various fields of human endeavor, and improve your transaction experience. Welcome to the new speed of economy—blockchain—but before we discuss this subject, I have this amazing welcome gift for you. It would be great if you could join my inner circle so that we can stay in touch and you can start receiving my new books at a discounted price. I want to give you an amazing reader experience. I have a special offer ready for you on the next page.

Cryptocurrency Secrets + Newsletter

Join my **FREE** Cryptocurrency Newsletter to start receiving more information related to everything FinTech. It will help you stay on track, and you will also be notified about my new books (at a special discounted price).

The best part? When you subscribe, you will immediately receive my ***Cryptocurrency Secrets*** report, where you will discover exciting content, such as *The type of cryptocurrencies available, strategies for investing, how to collect more bitcoin, and much more!* It's just my way of saying thank you for your readership!

Follow The Link Below To Subscribe And Get Free Instant Access:

cryptocurrencystudio.com/offer

Chapter 1: Getting Started With Blockchain

What is Blockchain?

Simply put, blockchain is a technology that simplifies our transactions. It is a numerical or digital (online) ledger that records transactions that are made in cryptocurrencies, sequentially and openly. It is different from the current way of banking, where all transactions are linked to a nonvisible, centralized network. Blockchain technology, however, is a decentralized database of the digital ledger that is made public for all to see. It makes it possible to monitor every transaction in detail. Even in the comfort of your own room, you can control all your transactions transparently. Each transaction is viewed as a single block, where subsequent transactions or blocks are added to make a digital, linear, chronological chain known as a blockchain. Each time a block is completed, a new block is automatically generated. The records of this digital ledger cannot be altered or erased without altering a previous transaction or block, and any attempt to do this will result in disruption of the whole network. Each computer connected to this network is called a node. When a new transaction is recorded, a copy of the blockchain is sent to each node as they join the network. This decentralized database of the digital ledger is replicated and harmonized through the Internet by anyone connected, rendering useless the use of a centralized administrator (such as banks). This digital ledger is incorruptible (no centralized information is available for alteration or hacking), and it records not only financial dealing but also anything of value (assets).

This ensures that each node or computer connected to this decentralized network has all the information about every transaction from the beginning to the most recently completed transaction. All other forms of transactions need a third party or an intermediary for them to work. Middlemen perform simple tasks, such as keeping records and authenticating the transaction processes, but with blockchain technology, you do not need a third party to conduct business. The money, property, and stocks are displayed on the computer as files. Re-creating such files is much easier, and you don't need a middleman in the whole process at all.

This technology allows people to trust each other, thereby extending the borders of the transaction. It is also safe, as hacking the system is unfathomable. For example, if someone wants to hack into a single transaction or block, he will not just try to alter that block but also the previous block and then the previous block back to the very beginning of the transaction. What's worse is that he will then try to gain access to all the computers connected to that network, which could number in the millions. Accordingly, the possibility of someone hacking into the system is very low as opposed to the centralized systems we have today. There have been cases of banking systems being hacked, identities stolen, and bank records cleared. None of these are possible with blockchain technology.

We can further illustrate blockchain this way: Mr. A and Mr. B placed a bet of $10 each on whether or not it will rain the next day, where the winner pockets $20. They can decide to keep the $20 with a third party until the next day when the winner expects to get his reward. The third party can be influenced or swayed by sentiment if Mr. A wins, but he is close to Mr. B and vice versa. What if they eliminate the third party and drop the $20 into an automated machine that automatically credits the winner? Another example is comparing how information is shared through Microsoft Word documents. If Mr. A sends a Microsoft document to Mr. B to make an adjustment, Mr. A needs to wait until he receives a return copy from Mr. B before viewing the changes made to the document. It is as if the document is temporarily locked out of Mr. A's sight. But what if there were a platform, such as Google Docs or Spreadsheet, that grants Mr. A and Mr. B access to that same document at the same time? When one of them is making a correction, this same information is shared with the other, and both can view it simultaneously. It is like a shared digital ledger between them and will be available to others who connect to that network.

These two different examples are exactly what blockchain does. No third party—just plain transparency, instant access, and assured expectation. Vitali Buterin made the following comments about blockchain: "A blockchain is a magic computer that anyone can upload programs to and leave the programs to self-execute, where the current and all previous states of every program are always visible, and which carries a very strong crypto economically secured guarantee that programs running on the chain will continue to execute in exactly the way that the blockchain protocol specifies."

Want more? The relationship between blockchain technology and cryptocurrencies (e.g., bitcoin) has been likened to what the Internet is to email. It will have a very great impact on the next generation. It gives all who are connected to the network equal access unlike banks and governments today. Eliminating intermediaries makes it possible to conduct transactions with more frequency and efficiency, contributing to foreseeable high traffic in local and international trades. It will allow more freedom as well, as many countries spend millions of dollars fighting corruption. With blockchain technology, though, protection against exploitation and corruption is guaranteed. Even the high number of people who lack exposure to the global economy will now be more familiar with payment and financial systems. Blockchain is no doubt the blueprint for all cryptocurrencies.

The History of Blockchain

When discussing the history of the blockchain, someone known as Satoshi Nakamoto must be mentioned. He was an anonymous scientist whose work, a 9-page white paper, was published almost a decade ago (2008 precisely). His work is almost an unbelievable postulation. He gave a rough draft in detail on how to make cryptocurrency that is powered by a complex mathematical formula and irrepressible distributed plan. Bitcoin will be discussed in detail later in this book, but we must mention it briefly at this point. In Santoshi's white paper, he explained how bitcoin can serve as a financial payment method between two willing parties, without a need for a third party regularizing the transaction. He postulated that each transaction will be stored in a digital ledger (the blockchain), with each recent block or transaction connected or added to a preceding block and the preceding block to another preceding block, in that order, to form a chain of blocks or transaction, using a digital signature. It is going to be built on trust and transparency because participants can authenticate the signatures by running various sophisticated algorithms. In this way, they can add blocks or transactions to the blockchain. In this system, two people who are not familiar with each other can exchange values through the network with full confidence that they will not be victims of any financial mishap.

Basically, blockchain technology was introduced when the bitcoin was invented in 2008, but implementation did not begin until 2009. Many argue that this theory of digital currency is new, but the concept of electronic money is not strange. We remember quite vividly the name David Chaum, who in the 1980s proposed a model of e-cash modus operandi. In the last ten years, however, a series of inventions have proved pivotal for achieving what was once considered a dream.

- The first invention was the bitcoin. It started as a digital tryout, but as of mid-2017, the market capitalization of bitcoin is now $38,803,254,566 at the rate of $2,423.78 and a circulating supply of 16,421, 975 BTC and volume (24h) at $759,340,000. Amazing, isn't it? In just ten years of innovation? Who knows what the future holds. Millions of people across

the globe use this medium of payment, making both large and growing remittances.
- The next invention is the blockchain, which is considered the blueprint, the technology that operated cryptocurrencies like the bitcoin. This innovation has been seen to be useful not just with the currency but also in other fields of human endeavor. Since its innovation, almost all financial organizations throughout the world have begun researching how they can harness this useful technology. According to IBM (International Business Machines Corporation), it is believed that blockchain will be used by 15% of the world's major banks worldwide by 2017, and the number is expected to rise to 65% by 2019.
- The next invention is the Smart Contract expressed by the creation of another kind of cryptocurrency called the Ethereum. It creates computer programs straight into blockchain, and this computer program provides a platform different from that of the bitcoin. The bitcoin represented cashlike tokens, but the ethereum allowed financial tools to be

represented instead. Since its invention date, it has been graced by millions of people. Smart contracts boast a market capitalization of $25,266,094,727 at the rate of $271.82 with a circulating supply of 92,951224ETH with a volume (24h) of $1,071,180,000.

- The next invention is the "Proof of stake," which is considered the most recent modern stage of blockchain thinking. Currently, cryptocurrencies, like the bitcoin, are secured by "proof of work," which simply means that the group that makes the decisions is the group with the largest computing power. These groups that are responsible for the decision-making are known as the "miners." They provide security by operating vast data in exchange for cryptocurrency payments. The "Proof of stake" system, however, does not make use of vast data centers; rather, it uses sophisticated financial tools for a higher degree of security. The proof-of-stake system is expected to go mainstream in 2017.
- The fifth invention is the blockchain scaling. Currently, all computers connected to the

blockchain network work together to process every transaction. To be sincere, this is quite slow. What if there were a faster medium of processing transactions? A scaled blockchain provides the answer. It speeds up the process without jeopardizing security. It calculates how many computers are needed to execute a transaction and divides labor among the computers, so the overall output can be more efficient and also faster. It will no doubt be fast enough to go head-to-head with the current major middlemen in the financial world while powering the Internet as well.

As this progressive innovation hits the market, it is expected that rapid changes will take place. An example is for the transaction to go from taking days to execute to complete within hours, a few minutes, even immediately. The cost of processing each transaction is also expected to drop. In fact, we can't really predict its full impact because predictors often fall into underestimating long-term effects as well as overestimating how fast a change can affect the economy, but we are sure that it will surely improve the face of business.

Many government agencies are ready to start using it full time. For example, Dubai already has a blockchain strategy. They plan to start issuing all government documents on blockchain by at least 2020, and owing to its success, it is expected that many other government agencies will follow suit. It will start a global transformation in trading and partnership. In the book *The Entrepreneur State*, Mariana Mazzucato teaches that blockchain technology will be the leading edge of innovation, particularly in infrastructure, and it is often in the hands of the state, and that seems destined to be true in the blockchain space.

What You Need to Know About Cryptocurrency

As was discussed earlier in this chapter, cryptocurrency is a digital type of currency that makes use of encryption to carry out and verify/validate transactions. We remember that as each block or transaction is completed it is automatically added to previously existing blocks to make a chain of blocks or transaction known as blockchain. We also note that cryptocurrency is supported by top governments, including the USA, and under consideration by some other notable governments, such as Argentina, Brazil, and Cyprus, as an alternative to fiat currencies.

What is a Cryptocurrency Address?

Just as a literal address helps others locate and confirm your ownership of a property so does the cryptocurrency address. It is unique for every customer. It is a public address that utilizes a number of unique characters to receive cryptocurrencies. It proves your ownership because each public address has a corresponding private address linked to it, and this private address is also linked to the digital ledger, the blockchain. It is just like a special mailbox through which you receive currency instead of emails.

Concept of a Digital Wallet

Everyone loves to own a wallet, which can be used to hold some cash maybe of different dominations for transactional purposes when needed. When dealing in cryptocurrencies, the digital type of currencies, you may start thinking of a central domain that stores your assets, but a digital wallet does more than hold cash.

A digital wallet is an electronic device that permits all forms of electronic transactions, be it purchasing items online or at a store. It can be used from a personal or shared computer or even from your smartphone. Even your bank account can be linked to your digital wallet. It can also be used to store digital coupons or loyalty card information. No more long queues and hours of delays you ask? Life made easy? Exactly! Conducting transactions, making and receiving payments, interaction with merchants worldwide, and liaisons with business partners will be a lot easier thanks to this wonderful innovation, but you must be careful with digital wallets because many different types are available. You can't just choose any particular one, as each person and the type of business they do differs. While your financial adviser or your banking service can be of help in determining which one is right for the type of business that you do, it is not their responsibility to make the final decision. Since it is your responsibility to protect your money, property, and other financial assets, it is your sole responsibility to make the final decision as to choosing the type of digital wallet that will best help you to adopt good monetary practice.

Different Types of Cryptocurrencies

The bitcoin has become a household name since Satoshi Nakamoto created it, and when people hear about cryptocurrency, they automatically think of bitcoin. Actually, though, a cryptocurrency can be created at any time, and with the rate of growth that is now synonymous with cryptocurrency, it is expected to increase in the coming years. As of January 2015, more than five hundred different types of cryptocurrencies were present. As noted earlier, the largest and most successful cryptocurrency in the blockchain network is the bitcoin, but several others are worth mentioning. The bitcoin is followed closely by Ethereum, Ripple, and Litecoin respectively. Now some nine hundred types of cryptocurrencies are available, and the number is still growing. What follows is a discussion of the top ten types of cryptocurrencies and how they can benefit you, which should motivate you to think about trying this new innovation.

1. **Bitcoin**

    The bitcoin, which was created by the anonymous scientist Satoshi Nakamoto in 2008, is one of the pioneers of digital currency and can be used to purchase items over the Internet (electronically) and in some cases even locally. You really don't need to understand everything about the technicalities of the bitcoin before you can start using it as a means of exchange. Just install the bitcoin wallet on your electronic device—maybe a computer or a smartphone. It will automatically generate a bitcoin address for you once this is done, and then you can proceed to perform all types of real transactions with it. As your need for more transactions increases, you can generate more bitcoin addresses for yourself. For a full in-depth look into Bitcoin checkout my recent release "Bitcoin: The Complete Guide To Understanding Bitcoin" You can find it at http://cryptocurrencystudio.com/bitcoin

I constantly update all my books. With all the future updates I have planned to come soon I promise you'll love it! (All my crypto series)

2. **Ethereum**

This decentralized computing platform will foster trust even among strangers. You can do business with virtually anybody because with the ethereum all terms and conditions are clearly spelled out in a "smart contract," which is digitally registered on the blockchain network. This smart contract functionality offers the Eretheum Virtual Machine (EVM), a virtual machine that verifies and validates all contracts using a cryptocurrency known as "Ether." The embedded "smart contract" can be used several times for different transactions. No wonder its market capitalization as of 2017 is second on the cryptocurrency table, with only bitcoin ahead of it. For a full in-depth look into Ethereum please checkout "Ethereum: The Complete Guide To Understanding Ethereum" You can find it at:

http://cryptocurrencystudio.com/ethereum

3. Ripple

It is also known as the Ripple Transaction Protocol (RTXP), and as expected it is built on an open source (decentralized) Internet protocol and currency known as Ripples (XRP). This Ripple protocol uses an agreed-upon process to facilitate all transactions, be it an exchange, payments, or withdrawals. It is easy to understand and use, as it offers instant, cost-effective payments, both locally and internationally. It was launched in 2013.

4. **Litecoin**

   Launched in 2011, this digital currency is almost identical to the bitcoin. Some even argue that its creation was inspired by the bitcoin. The transfer policy was built on an open source protocol as well. It is a peer-to-peer cryptocurrency that was released under the MIT (X11) software license.

5. **Dash (formally known as Darkcoin)**

   This digital currency was launched by Evan Duffield in 2014. It is a more secretive form of bitcoin, as its formal name, Darkcoin, shows. Business dealings are almost untraceable, as it provides more added privacy. During its launch, two key features of this cryptocurrency that were emphasized were privacy and speed. It has since lived up to its expectations, and "dash" has an ever-growing fan base.

6. **Peercoin**

This one-of-its-kind digital currency was created by Scott Nadal and Sunny King, two software developers, in 2012. Its most unique feature is its combination of "proof-of-work" and "proof-of-stake." It was formally known as PPcoin. The "proof-of-work" hashing process used in mining this coin was initially difficult, but to make up for this, users were rewarded with coins that used the "proof-of-stake" algorithm. The advantage of this remodeled coin is that it requires little energy to generate blocks or, in other words, complete a transaction.

7. **Dogecoin**

This digital currency was launched in 2013 and uses a technology of scripts as a proof-of-work scheme. The makeup was based on the same protocol used in creating the bitcoin, although there were some modifications. There is no limit to the production of this digital currency, which is best suited for carrying out smaller transactions because it deals with coins that are of lesser value individually. The block time is approximately sixty seconds.

8. **Primecoin**

    In the summer of 2013, software developer Sunny King developed this digital currency. Its technicality, which is the proof-of-work, was based on prime numbers, which is completely different from the bitcoin framework. It works to find unique long chains of prime numbers, thereby providing greater mining ease and added network security.

9. **Chinacoin**

    This currency is based on the same framework as with the Litecoin. It uses the script key derivation function, which is password based. It is generated in a block of sixty seconds, with eighty-eight coins per block. Amazing!

10. **Ven**

    This digital currency was launched in 2007. It was created to reduce the risk of inflation. Its value in the financial market is determined from a list of currencies, commodities, and carbon features.

As these reviews show, cryptocurrency is not all about bitcoin. In fact, the well-known bitcoin has alternatives, such as the Auroracoin, Mastercoin, Freicoin, Quark, Sexcoin, and Namecoin. You can also choose from a host of other types of digital currencies. Based on CoinMarketCap.com, a website that regularly publishes the market capitalization of cryptocurrencies, about twenty types of digital currencies are available that sell for more than $1. For a full in-depth look into cryptocurrency please check out "Cryptocurrency: The Complete Guide To Understanding Cryptocurrency". You can find it at: http://www.cryptocurrencystudio.com/cryptocurrency

Chapter 2: Current World of Blockchain

Blockchain Mining and Investment

Blockchain Mining

In this article, we will use the bitcoin as a case study of digital currencies. As you read about bitcoin mining, remember that the bigger picture of this discussion is the blockchain and its mining. Basically, mining in this context refers to the addition of new block records (transactions) to the public ledger of blocks. We remember that these blocks make up a chain of transactions or blocks in that digital ledger known as the blockchain. Once these records are recorded, the blockchain makes it public to other connected networks or nodes of the completed block. The node connected to the blockchain makes use of this information in differentiating between legitimate and illegal bitcoin transactions and from attempts to respend coins that have already been spent. Since the bitcoin uses the "proof-of-work" function, each transaction or block must contain this hashcash "proof-of-work" for it to be considered authentic and acceptable. When the blockchain receives a new block, each node connected to the blockchain tries to verify this block's "proof-of-work" and then on completion of this verification, validates the block or transaction. It only takes a few seconds to complete this process. Upon validation, the new block is added. In this way, the number of blocks added each day is kept in check and remains steady. It is resource intensive and was specifically designed for this purpose. It allows each blockchain connected node to keep transactions secure and reach a tamper-resistant agreement.

But mining is also used to introduce new digital currency into the system. When new coins are created, miners are rewarded with transaction fees. These new coins are distributed in a decentralized manner, which builds confidence in the security of the entire system. Miners of cryptocurrencies assist in keeping the network secure by a consensus approval of transactions. Mining ensures fairness while keeping the network safe, secure, and stable.

How does the mining process work? Let us briefly take a look at the way hard currency or paper money is circulated as an example. The government decides and then approves when to print cash and how to distribute it. In this respect, though, the bitcoin does not need a central government to approve its creation and circulation. It is a digital, decentralized currency that does not need a central government to be involved. Miners use specialized software programs and specially designed mining hardware to create or mine these currencies. They use the software programs to solve arithmetic problems and in exchange are issued a set number of digital currencies. It is a smart way to get the currencies and also encouraging to others who are interested in mining these digital currencies.

Blockchain Mining Hardware

Hardware for mining cryptocurrency is designed to generate "proof-of-work." There is much hardware to choose from, but your choice will be determined by a number of factors, including the type of coin you want, hashing algorithm, and the general acceptability of the hardware in terms of users' ratings. What exactly is the above-mentioned hashing algorithm or hashrate? It is the rate that controls how many attempts a miner makes in solving a cryptocurrency block per second. The more attempts at solving a cryptocurrency block, the greater the chances of solving the block and the better the mining hardware. The hashrate is measured in hash per second (H/s). We can have Kilohash (KH/s), Megahash (MH/s), Gigahash (GH/s), Tetrahash (TH/s), and Petahash (PH/s). Shown below is a table that provides details about hardware for the top three cryptocurrencies.

Harware name	Avalon 6	AntMiner S7	AntMiner S9
Hashrate	3.5 TH/s	4.73 TH/s	11.8 TH/s
Power usage	1050 watts	1350 watts	1350 watts
Power efficiency	0.29 Joules per GH	0.28 Joules per GH	0.1 Joules per GH
Controller	Separate	Built-in	Built-in
Noise	55 db	62 db	50 db
Chip process	28 nm	28 nm	16 nm
Breakeven point	7 years	2.6 Years	0.9 Years

You have a wide choice of hardware to choose from. If you think of mining, the ones above are the most recommended.

Blockchain Mining Software

The major work of creating a digital currency is done by the mining hardware, but mining software is also indispensable. It is needed to link the mining hardware to the blockchain network. Just as with the hardware, a number of factors must be considered in choosing which software program will be useful for you in your cryptocurrency mining process. These factors include the operating system and the type of cryptocurrency you plan to create. As discussed in the preceding chapter, upwards of nine hundred different types of digital currencies were available as of 2017, and each of these has specialized software for it, which means that if you are planning on creating Litecoin, for example, the software used in the creation of Dogecoin may not work for you. It must be noted, though, that some software can be used to create more than one type of cryptocurrency. Below are some examples of software programs from which you can choose.

Example:

- ZOTAC 750 T 1GB (5.35 MH/s for Lyra 2v2)
- XFX 7990 (21.8 MH/s for x11)
- XFX 7990 (28 MH/S for Quark)
- XFX R9 290x black edition (32 MH/s for Ethash)

Mining Difficulty

Simply stated, this is a measure of difficulty in finding a new block or how difficult it is to find a hash below a given target. The measure is periodically adjusted based on the hashing power that has been deployed by connected miners. There is a global block difficulty, so blocks that are considered valid must hash below this target. The difficulty is adjusted every 2,016 blocks, based on the time taken to find the previous 2,016 blocks. If one block is discovered every ten minutes, it will take two weeks to find 2,016 blocks. If the previous 2,016 blocks took longer than two weeks to find, the difficulty is reduced. Conversely, if it took less than two weeks to find 2,016 blocks, as expected the difficulty is increased.

Blockchain Investment

With all this information available, it is only logical to wonder how you can invest in this ever growing economy of the blockchain. You might want to ask such questions as What do I need to do to not lose money? What do I need to know? When is the right time to invest, and how can I make the best possible profit?

You should invest in blockchain because it is the fastest-growing investment opportunity presently available. Every day the number of network users is steadily growing at an exponential rate, which, in turn, leads to positive growth of the investment. Let us consider Facebook. Currently, it is worth over $30 billion. It is growing every day. More than six billion people currently use it, and every insightful business owner wants to invest in it. Why? Only three steps are involved: invest, wait, and profit. The same is true of the blockchain technology. Consider these statistics:

In 2010, there were only about 10,000 users. In 2012, the number increased to 100,000. Two years later in 2014 the number of users jumped to 1,000,000, and last year a record 10,000,000 users were recorded. With this rate, in 2020, it is estimated that about 100,000,000 users will be actively using blockchain technology. As the number of network users grow, so will the investment. No doubt now is the time to think about investing your money and just wait for your profit to roll in. It is the best investment opportunity now, and some have called it the best investment opportunity since the Internet. Smart move!

Blockchain technology will eliminate financial deception in a number of ways. Banks can go bankrupt. Money can be lost even if it is kept in the bank, and if the bank's capital base is not large enough, all you will hear afterward is SORRY.

Blockchain technology, however, is a mathematical guarantor of economic freedom.

Before you think of investing, take time to get at least a basic knowledge of the computer and how to operate it. If you don't and want to invest in blockchain technology, you may well lose your hard-earned money.

Know also that all accounts require a password. Create one that you will easily remember, or better still, write it down so that you can easily go back to check in case you forget. Also be sure to choose a password that others cannot easily guess. You don't want your money in the wrong hands.

Learn to back up your data. If you have disliked using antivirus programs, learn to love them and regularly update them. This will protect your computer as well as your accounts.

In essence, before thinking about investing in crypto-economy, try to improve your computer literacy.

The next step is to sit down and determine what percentage of your income you want to invest. Realize that there are risks, especially as a new investor, and to be on a safe side, try to start with an investment of between 1% and 10% of your income. This is important, as expectations may not be met immediately, although the possibility of this is very low as long as you are computer literate. As you become familiar with the system, gradually increase your stake or investment.

Also be sure to note that the blockchain investment opportunity is a long-term trust. It yields interests and profits over time. If you are someone who wants instant profits, it is not for you. Reasonably define the investment period from the start to within three to eight years because blockchain is still in its embryonic stage.

Study the market, observe the trend, know when the tide is high or low, and determine when is the best time to buy or sell.

Useful Tips From Experts for Cryptocurrency Miners and Users

Succeeding on the blockchain network requires careful study and calculation, but appreciate all the useful ideas and tips from those who have been successful in trading with cryptocurrencies. It is like planning a journey to a distant land you have never been to before. You may not know what to expect, but if someone who has been there before gives you firsthand information about the place, their culture, and living conditions, you will be more confident of going there. What may at first seem a dangerous quest will in no time turn into an interesting, mouthwatering adventure. In this article, we will take a look at what has made some hit the jackpot with cryptocurrency. We will also explain how you can make use of the tips therein.

Privacy Tips

One important point for all blockchain users is being able to surf the Internet and conduct dealings with a considerable standard of privacy. People trade every day in digital currencies amounting to millions of dollars. We know our personal business dealings is no one else's business, hence our need for increased privacy. Since the digital ledger, the blockchain, is usually visible to all connected nodes, movement of funds is also well known to others. This can pose a threat to our public online dealings and can leave us susceptible to various malicious groups whose aim is to keep track of users and their online activities.

Hackers also pose a risk, and how can we really differentiate between hackers and genuine business partners when we cannot meet on a personal level? We need to protect ourselves. Shown below are three things you can do to increase your online security.

- Connect to a proxy
- Browse on TOR
- Get a Virtual Privacy Network (VPN)

Each security strategy has its advantages and disadvantages, costs and limitations, strengths and weaknesses. Here is a brief discussion of three online security options. You should be able to make an informed decision afterward as to how you can increase your online privacy.

Proxy Security

We have known about proxies for quite some time. What is a proxy? It is a device that is set up in a location that Internet users can bounce their connection off of before the rest of the Net. Proxies are the first innovation of the Internet in setting up a remote connection, but how can they protect your online business dealings? They provide security or privacy by acting more like a firewall and prevent unauthorized intrusion, thereby hosting very meaningful security, but some have based routers that offer better security than the normal proxies. Many proxies are free, but in terms of Internet security, free is not always good. Free is not always secure or reliable. Free in the world of online privacy can mean less bandwidth and weak security. They can assume a different IP address for some procedures, but for resisting some more advanced tracking, they can be found wanting. If you are a user on a very tight budget, proxy security is for you, but do note that they offer limited security.

Browse on TOR

TOR means The Onion Router. It works to make your connection masked from close monitoring by running many different relays. Each of these connections makes it very hard to trace every action back to the IP address generating those actions. It is like a series of proxies working together. The TOR browser is free to install and has an IOS version as well as an Android version. Some government agencies with a very high IT strength (for example, the CIA and the NSA) will still be able to track you because they can tell if you are using a TOR browser. Even though it is free, it still does a great job.

Virtual Private Network (VPN)

Of the three security options, the VPN is the best for enhancing your online privacy at any given time. This is because VPNs are encrypted, and if you are using an encrypted command, so is your online activity. VPN handles all Internet traffic with ease, and it is not attached to a specific application or browser. The TOR browser has a limited scope of activities, but with VPN, your entire Internet connection is protected, and you do not need to worry if you can or cannot engage in some particular activities. It is premium, though, which means you have to pay for it—but one thing is guaranteed. It offers the best online protection. To choose the best VPN, here are a number of factors to consider:

- Cost and speed
- Effectiveness of their customer service
- Do they keep logs?
- What devices are supported?

The location of the VPN host is another factor to consider, which is important because most of us like being incognito when we are online. Depending on the location of some VPN hosts, some governments might force certain hosts to submit a record of their tracking activities. Since you are paying for such services, you expect the best treatment, and you deserve the best. Choose a VPN host that guarantees a good customer care relationship. Good customer service is identified by the means of contact the VPN host supports. Ideally, a good customer service should support phone, email, and chat as basic means of contact. If the host you are considering offers anything less, consider changing your decision. Some VPN can work on the iOS platform, while others can work with Android devices. Another factor to consider is if the VPN host allows several connections. With a single subscription, you should be able to connect different devices. It will be less acceptable if you have to pay for a subscription with every device you use.

Other Useful Tips
1. Take advantage of all the resources that you can. Some people take the various Internet search engines for granted. What do you have to lose? Take time to walk yourself through the fundamentals by doing a quick search every now and then regarding questions you have about blockchain trading. You will be surprised to know how much you will learn. You will confidently and easily trade alongside pros in the business and will readily be on hand to provide help for those who need it.
2. Write down your wallet recovery phase, wallet ID, and password. Store them where you are sure they cannot be easily lost before attempting to send funds to your wallet. The wallet recovery phase helps to back up your data. Other tips might suggest how to protect your online activities from other people, but the wallet recovery phase is like protection against yourself. When you are setting up your wallet, you can always back up your wallet. Do not skip this

section, as it could be very crucial to your success. Two types of keys are associated with your wallet: a public key and a private key. This wallet recovery phase will ensure that these keys are saved into your file. As long as the keys are saved, the blockchain network will be able to retrieve your balance with ease and at any time. You can store the keys in any external storage of your choice, be it portable, external hard drive, a flash drive, an optical disk, a mobile phone, or even on a piece of paper in written form. It can also be stored on a cloud-based system of backups like the icloud on iOS devices or Dropbox in Android and Windows devices, but the cloud storage system is not 100% reliable. It is recommended that you encrypt the data before uploading it to any cloud-based storage medium.

3. Always double-check your transaction details before hitting the "Enter" button and sending. It is all too common for us to double-check a bank statement before giving it to the cashier, even though a

mistake can be reversed if it is noticed. If we can make such efforts with bank statements, it is all the more important to double-check online transactions in the blockchain networks before sending them. The reason is simple. Once you hit the "Send" button, it can never be reversed. It is imperative to double-check the amount of digital currency you want to send so that you know you are sending the right amount. Also be sure to double-check the cryptocurrency address you intend to send to. You don't want to make a mistake.

4. Keep separate wallets. A person can create and keep as many digital wallets as they prefer, as there is no limit to the number of wallets you can create. If your entire digital currency holdings is in a single wallet, you may be vulnerable to all sorts of online abuse. Some experts and professionals keep separate digital wallets for different purposes. They have a separate wallet for making remittances and sending money, a separate wallet for receiving payments, and

another for their savings. You can adopt this method that is sure to work for you too.

5. It will do you some good not to keep all your savings in a web wallet. A web wallet is certainly convenient to own and maintain, but it should be operated like a checking account (where we store only money we plan to use soon). Learn to handle your web wallet the same way. Some web wallets have been hacked. For your protection, only a limited amount of spending money should be kept in your web wallet. If your wallet is hacked, your loss will be limited. Always remember that if you lose money on the blockchain network, the money is simply gone. Even if you call the police and they try to help you by investigating, the chances of getting back your money are very low.

6. Do all you can to increase your online privacy. Do not get into the habit of sharing your passwords or keys with anyone. Your wallet address or your public key is like your bank account number, and your private key is like the PIN associated with

your account, through which transactions with that account number are validated. Do not reveal your financial details to hackers. This information should always be kept to yourself. Always avoid being too familiar with strangers. Since blockchain technology is visible to all connected nodes, it is easy to trust business partners that we don't see. If you get too familiar, though, chances are they will start investigating how much your holdings are worth. One thing you can do is try to conceal relations between your separate wallets (i.e., between your spending wallet and your saving wallet) by transferring funds between them using a mixing service or programs that protect your privacy and anonymity.

7. Even if you keep your digital currency holdings in a wallet stored in a device like a computer, it does not mean you are totally protected from attacks. Different viruses and malware can infect computers, like the Trojan horse. That is why you must get a good antivirus program. Also, try storing

your wallet's private key in an offline medium, which is another measure of protection against attacks. It could be on a flash drive or USB key. You can also encrypt your private key so that in case it falls into the wrong hands it will be useless, as it cannot be used without decrypting it, and to do that, your password is needed. If you decide to encrypt your private key, do not forget your password, as even you can be barred from access to your digital wallet.

Latest News and Information Regarding Blockchain

Blockchain has made great strides within the last decade, and this industry is just getting started. The following articles will help you get the latest groundbreaking information about blockchain technology.

1. **Fox Business Foretells Bitcoin Price Could Reach $1 Billion (6/7/2017)**: Throughout the first two quarters of 2017, the price of bitcoin has risen to the extent that there is a redefined awareness in

cryptocurrency from the media. Before now, the press has been quite negative about the financial prospects of investing in the blockchain, but a great many people understand that bitcoin and other forms of digital currency are an enduring financial and technological force. Recently, Jim Cramer, a CNBC personality, suggested that the bitcoin price could rise to $1 million as a result of ransomware attacks. Also, a Fox business show asked whether the price of bitcoin could reach 1$ billion. On June 30, 2017, Charles Payne in his show *Making Money with Charles Payne* featured Naomi Brockwell (former New York Bitcoin Center Policy Director). Naomi attributed the recent increase in the price of bitcoin to the political ramifications of its decentralized nature. She said that people living in lands under very harsh regimes can use the bitcoin to purchase food and other products not available in their countries. She said, "The main people promoting this technology are those who understand that the government can be dangerous." Although no one directly said the price of bitcoin could rise to $1 billion, when she was asked if the bitcoin price could reach $1 billion, she agreed and said it could go "to the moon."

2. **22 Global Banks Will Test SWIFT's Cross-Border Payments Blockchain (6/7/2017):** The operator of the platform used by the global banking system SWIFT has included twenty-two new banks to its ongoing blockchain proof-of-concept. SWIFT has labeled this ongoing project as "the new standard for cross-border payments." In an announcement on July 6, 2017, SWIFT confirmed the addition of these new banks to this blockchain endeavor. The PoC blockchain movement was initially founded by six banks back in April. Hyperledger Fabric was chosen as the core technology of this trial. Why the trial? SWIFT announced in April that the purpose of the trial is to help banks reconcile with

their international Nostro accounts in real time. These accounts help banking systems to remit money in designated Nostro accounts globally. These doctor accounts make possible international money transfers. Damien Vandervsken, head of R&D of SWIFTLab and user experience at SWIFT said: "If banks could manage their Nostro account liquidity in real time, it would allow them to accurately gauge how much money is required in each account at any given point, ultimately enabling them to free up significant funds for other investments." The twenty-two banks are major banks from Africa, Asia, Europe, and North America. These banks will work together as a group to help validate the blockchain test application developed by the six original banks.

3. **India Becomes a Breeding Ground for Blockchain Engineers (6/7/2017):** India is emerging as a talent pool of blockchain engineers because of the rising

global demand for blockchain technology. Students and professionals in India are quickly signing up for courses related to blockchain to help them develop or acquire the needed technical skills to start their research in this innovation and possibly adopt it. The *Times of India* (India's biggest English-language newspaper) of July 6, 2017, revealed that e-learning marketplace Udemy recorded a 978% enrollment for courses related to blockchain, and of these new enrollments, an average of 80% are from India. This has no doubt fueled their interest in cryptocurrency. With a margin of about 40%, India leads Australia as the largest pool of talent in the Asia-Pacific region.

4. **IOTA Partners Healthcare Providers for Blockchain Research in Norway (6/7/2017)**: For about a year now, the IOTA Foundation has been making a concerted effort in applying its Tangle distributed ledger network to the public,

with a focus on eHealth. The foundation is presently partnering with top Norwegian healthcare providers, such as Oslo Medtech, the Norwegian Centre for eHealth Research, and the Oslo Cancer Cluster. The partnership is expected to form a Distributed Ledger Technology research network. Norway is known for its fast adoption of new policies, as it was one of the leading countries to start racing toward a fully cashless policy. With this move by IOTA, machine learning will be used to improve diagnostics and quick cancer detection; social media will be used to predict the spread of flu. No wonder many industries are exploring blockchain and distributed ledger technology as a means to continue developing. It is expected that other countries will follow suit.

5. **A New Pro-Bitcoin Ethereum Association Launches in the German Parliament (6/30/2017)**: There is a new blockchain and nationwide federal digital

currency lobby group known as the "Bundesverband"—the Federal Blockchain Association in Germany. This official recognition, with just a number of attendees from the German members of Parliament, took place in Germany's parliament building. An official release from the group stated that "Blockchain will be the basic technology for the next innovation stage of the Internet, and Germany has a chance to put itself at the forefront of the world through pioneering regulation. The Federal Association is to help seize this opportunity."

6. **Delaware Passes Groundbreaking Blockchain Regulation Bill (7/7/2017):** The state of Delaware has passed a bill that recognizes as law the trading of stocks on blockchain technology. In April it was reported that the Corporation Law Section of the Delaware State Bar Association (DSBA) had approved Delaware Law Amendments with the

intention of delivering statutory authority for businesses in the state to use the blockchain to maintain corporate records. According to the recent passage of Senate Bill 69, it states: "Amendments to Sections 219, 224, and 232 and related provisions are intended to provide specific statutory authority for Delaware corporations to use networks of electronic databases (examples of which are described currently as 'distributed ledgers' or a 'blockchain') for the creation and maintenance of corporate records, including the corporation's stock ledger." Passing the House at the end of June, the blockchain bill only received one vote against it out of a total of forty-one votes. With the advancement of the bill, it means that middlemen between sellers and buyers of stock could, essentially, be cut out of the process, providing faster settlement times. Origination of the bill was brought about last May when Jack Markell, then governor, announced an initiative to embrace the blockchain and smart contract technology. It was also hoped that it would provide a legal and regulatory environment for the development of the technology in the state and also help attract blockchain companies to Delaware.

7. **Blockchain Enables Indian Insurer Settle Motor, Travel Claims in Minutes (7/7/2017)**: In deploying blockchain-powered insurance products for travelers and vehicle owners, Indian insurer Bajaj Allianz General Insurance is hastening the claim settlement process from "days to minutes." Private insurance firm Bajaj Allianz is now deploying blockchain-based insurance products in the travel and motor sectors according to the Hindu Business Line. This will result in a seamless process of an otherwise cumbersome procedure of an insurance claim for end users. With "Travel Ezee," Bajaj Allianz is using innovative decentralized technology to proactively inform overseas travel policyholders of their payout eligibility in

the event of flight delays. The traditional process of a claim typically sees the user register a claim before submitting a certificate of delay from the airline. With blockchain technology, customers will be able to instantly receive their claims without needing to file any flight delay forms. Sourabh Chatterjee, head of IT at Bajaj Allianz, told the publication: "This is helping us to bring down the current settlement turnaround time for some plans from days to minutes."

Many other stories appear in newspapers every day that clearly show that blockchain technology is more than just a myth as some say. It is the next big thing happening.

Cryptocurrency Legalities, Taxes, and Regulations

Legal and Regulatory Issues Surrounding Blockchain Technology

The transparency and freedom associated with blockchain technology are the major attractive features of this new innovation, and many businesses, organizations, and individuals are getting ready to come on board. The decentralized order of events, however, does give rise to a number of questions concerning regulatory bodies and policymakers, both locally and internationally. It is true that many people are excited and optimistic about it, as they feel it will help improve customer compliance with regulations, tracking, and reporting, but other people and authorities are adopting a "let's wait and see" attitude.

Blockchain technology and the entire concept of digital economy has had its own challenges, including Blockchain latency, scalability, lack of exclusive reliance on digital commerce by some sectors, lack of sufficient information giving rise to a lack of understanding of what Blockchain can offer by the masses, and overreliance on the current legacy system that would eventually need to be done away with should the distributed ledger become the new system in place, among some other challenges. From a regulatory and legal point of view, the move to adopt this growing innovation will be like trying to negotiate a large-scale IT development. A few other regulatory challenges should be mentioned:

- **Accountability and Responsibility**—Since the digital ledger is going to be distributed among all connected nodes, the question still remains: Who is responsible for controlling or regulating this digital ledger? Who will regulate the users and any other connected party? In this decentralized system, if there happens to be a problem, who should be held accountable? Who even knows what or whom to regulate?
- **Who Will Regulate**—The Blockchain network remains in a cross-border initiative as we all know, without a central government determining what would be done as it was or acting as a regulatory body. Without international agreed-upon regulatory principles and cooperation, it is still something many are wondering how this will bring about a measure of cohesion in the economy.
- **Competition and Antitrust**—If this distributed ledger is eventually implemented, there could be arguments of cartel activity. Others will also argue that there may be risks that an algorithm will be set up such that it will

produce an anticompetitive result that cannot be easily detected.
- **Smart Contracts**—How will existing contract laws adapt to take into consideration the automated Smart contracts? Will they ever be considered valid and subsequently enforceable?
- **Privacy and Security**— Records will almost be impossible to decrypt, and the technology relies heavily on assumptions that it is very secure, but with the way computing has been developing in recent years that may not always be the case. This could raise some legitimate security concerns. For example, party identity from completed transactions could be traced by another party that has permission to decrypt data.

The blockchain has been tipped by experts to have the potential to transform virtually all sectors, and a number of organizations are already considering adopting this in not just their businesses but also in their dealings in other fields. Does that mean that blockchain technology is infallible? No. The challenges discussed above are still cause for concern.

With this on your mind, every organization will do well to deal with these raised issues as well as the regulatory challenges before proceeding to adopt it.

It also seems that most governments do not really understand how blockchain technology can help them. One typical example is with the Federation of Russia that announced in the first week of May 2017 that by 2019 they will have regulations guiding blockchain investment already in place, but they did not provide any further details regarding how these regulations will be implemented. It seems like good and interesting news, but that announcement in itself still highlights a measure of ignorance and a lack of the necessary understanding of the prospects that blockchain technology offers. While we are not faulting this move by this great nation, realistically speaking, an evolving technology like blockchain cannot be predicted, let alone give assurances of regulations within a set period of time. Such promises may never be kept.

Back in May, something happened at the European Parliament that was an entirely different approach. The gathering focused on the discovery of this technology rather than assurance of regulations. They focused more on what the technology can help us achieve and how it can be useful to the government. They later discussed ways in which they can help in developing it and concluded on ways to protect their customers. That sounded like a more realistic approach and shows the group really understands what blockchain technology can do. One problem still remains. Regulatory bodies that are set up will still have to think about what to regulate and whom to regulate.

Regulating software is very delicate because rules exist to regulate intended behavior. Another issue that can come up is deciding whether or not to let the market decide the regulatory parameters. A move promoting market rejection can render the technology's craftsmanship utterly irrelevant, but when the blockchain is used to transfer assets, waiting for the market to decide can have its own systematic consequences. Accordingly, there is also a need to regulate security measures.

Defining Blockchain Use

Even though we have identified different areas where this technology can be applied, we still don't know how extensive its applications will be in the coming years. What we do know about its applications so far is just the tip of the iceberg regarding what blockchain will offer in the future. The unusual division of private and public networks also requires a very different approach. While it is possible to draft laws governing the development of the private network, it is a different ball game regulating the public network based on their uses. It is really not going to be easy, taking into consideration the cross-border nature of this distribution. Laws will not be easy to establish and apply for it because blockchain, as we know, has no visible founder, let alone establishing its legal base. With the foregoing, it is clear that prospective regulators will only have the choice of "letting the market decide" when setting up regulations.

Blockchain Taxation in the USA

The date June 5, 2017, will live long in the memory of blockchain users. The state of Nevada became the first state in the USA to approve a bill that will restrain local government entities from taxing blockchain transactions. A significant portion of Nevada's revenue comes from entertainment, as the state is home to Las Vegas, the city of casinos that never sleeps. Concerning money, the state of Nevada is a revenue hub. With this legislative move, the state is opening the way for the success of blockchain technology.

The journey started on March 30 when Republican Senator Ben Kiechefer introduced Senate Bill 398, which was intended to protect blockchain transactions under the already existing electronic transaction act. The bill is the exact representation of blockchain technology. The bill states that it is "An electronic record of transaction or data which is

1. Uniformly ordered
2. Redundantly maintained or processed by one or more companies or machines to generate the consistency or non-repudiation of the recorded transaction data
3. Validation by using cryptography."

The bill was unanimously approved by the Senate in April, and when the Nevada Assembly moved in May, it was amended and sent back to the Senate to confirm its amendment. It was sent to Governor Brian Sandoval afterward and was finally approved. Senator Kiechefer later said, "The potential uses of blockchain are limitless, and I'm confident Nevada's entrepreneurs will find ways to use this technology to innovate and drive our economy forward. I can't wait to see what comes next."

On May 29, 2017, Arizona Governor Doug Ducey also signed a bill that recognized the loyalty of blockchain's signature and smart contracts. These examples provide just a glimpse of how large the influx of states and federation will be in eventually signing this technology into law and, most importantly, canceling government entities unnecessarily taxing blockchain transactions. A world centered on cryptocurrency is the future that we should look forward to. It is a doorway to more financial transparency and a better economy.

Chapter 3: Movement of the Future—Blockchain

Revolution of Banking and Marketing

Almost every international bank is trying out blockchain technology because of what it offers in terms of cost savings and operational efficiencies. These banks are experimenting with blockchain in a number of ways, such as building in-house solutions, partnering with fintechs, as well as membership in global consortia. Many banks are experimenting with using blockchain technology to modernize and simplify banking processes and reduce costs. Other reasons for wanting to try it include the ability to create fresh business models and the likelihood of competing with fintechs. They are also looking at how blockchain technology will help solve some problems they face on a daily basis in their businesses. Banking regulatory entities are also looking to use its framework for developing more efficient regulations. In fact, it will help speed up transactions and make them more secure.

The year 2015 was when major financial sectors started thinking about blockchain technology. It also stressed that financial organizations, such as banks, should use this technology to their advantage, teamwork, and partnership across the industry. It also highlighted that blockchain technology will help solve some key problems within the financial system, for example,

- Prevention of interference with an agreed-upon chain of transactions
- The issue of double spending
- Problems relating to trust
- Agreement on transaction history

Transparency is another feature of this technology that will benefit both the customers and the banking system. No one will be able to alter any record. In fact, it could save banks' infrastructure $20 billion a year by 2022.

Transactions today are often verified by a centralized system that keeps its own central ledger. This can slow down transactions, as it could take days to settle a deal. It can also take days for two or more banks to relate and agree with a particular customer's records. The blockchain initiative, however, will eliminate that waiting period, as each bank will have its own copy of the ledger immediately once the transactions are lodged. This will enable easy communication among participants. Transactions will be validated within seconds, and significant costs will be reduced.

Marketing will also be transformed. Many marketing procedures today may involve the use of intermediaries, many handovers, and lengthy processes. Applying blockchain technology will eliminate these problems.

What is also worth highlighting is that blockchain allows the use of "smart contracts," which will create a transaction route such that some actions will be approved automatically provided dome conditions are met. One example is as long as certain codes are complete, remittances will be approved.

In a new report *Beyond the hype: Blockchain in capital markets,* McKinsey says that the mainstream of the technology will advance in about four stages, starting with internal purpose-built distributed ledgers that operate within enterprises. This would be followed by the adoption of blockchain by a small subset of banks as an upgrade to manual processes, starting with assets that are traded infrequently and manually over the counter. This would help participants agree on standards and protocols for booking and transfer with relatively little investment. Next would involve conversion of inter-dealer settlements, which would help solidify the standardization of products, followed by a large-scale adoption across buyers and sellers in public markets, which McKinsey says ". . . would be a great leap forward and would depend on the large-scale conversion of existing systems and adoption by a large-scale number of market participants."

McKinsey makes four major recommendations for prompt action:

- Assess the effect on your business and plan for the long term.
- Participate in consortia and work with regulators. The payoff for cooperation over competition may be industry utilities and a faster development cycle.
- Capture the internal ledger opportunity: this would give individuals and firms the opportunity to test new technology on systems

already being revised and try to develop expertise without concern for network issues.
- Go after post-trade and manual processes. These can yield significant workflow benefits and be less disruptive to business models.

Considering the foregoing, it is clear that blockchain technology will improve banking services significantly, as these will mean great advantages to both regulators and customers, and marketing will be made very easy as well. Blockchain technology is the future of our current financial system. No wonder many refer to it as a needed revolution in marketing.

Securing Digital Identity
Whether the field of human endeavor involves work, business, leisure, politics, or healthcare, authorization of identities is directly connected to all of them, but the concept of identity authorization faces challenges perhaps because of inadequate common comprehension and the mostly unchecked cyberspace of personal information. Technology has advanced in recent times to pose a threat to digital identities, such as many more cases of hacked databases and account breaches. What blockchain does is use biometrics to

provide solutions to these issues concerning digital identity such that identities can be authorized uniquely in a manner that is unalterable, undeniable, and safe.

How exactly will blockchain technology help secure digital identity? We need to first consider how digital identities are represented in the blockchain. When a user's identity is entered into the blockchain network, it is seen as a self-asserted block that contains the user's identity feature. The block also contains the user's private and public keys. Other information that the user's block contains is electricity providers or banks along with their public keys or PINs for validation.

The user's relationship with the electricity provider is established by signing in with the public keys. Other relationships are gradually established between the user and the associated providers, and as more of these relationships are established within the blockchain network, confidence in the accuracy of the user's identity grows organically. As more transactions are completed in the name of that user, the "reputation capital" of that user's identity grows consistently.

In case one or more relationships between the user and the entities change, the difference is noted within the blockchain as a separate block with a unique cryptographically signed timestamp. This creates a cryptographically secured sequence that allows the new verifier to reconcile both previous and current relationships.

Rebranding Healthcare

Earlier in this book we mentioned how people in general and even experts don't know the full applications of blockchain technology. Over the years, some noticeable improvements have been made in healthcare owing to advancements in modern technology, which has led to an influx of innovative ideas as well as medical equipment and facilities. In spite of these improvements, however, the healthcare sector still faces challenges. Questions have been raised as to the industry's fidelity, efficiency, and general effectiveness. One example is the case of a patient who receives a wrong prescription medicine just because the hospital or healthcare provider is not aware of the complete medical record(s) of the patient. There are also reported cases (although not too common) where patients were transferred from one facility to another, and the new medical facility did not receive the transferred medical records in time to start immediate administering of treatment. These developments surely need reform. The entire healthcare system can be progressively changed for the better only if blockchain technology can be adopted. Outlined below are some changes that blockchain technology will bring to the healthcare industry.

1. **Data Exchange or Access to Data**: Let us use the prescription of a patient's medication as an example to explain this point. Normally, when a patient's medications are prescribed, different entities can fill out the form from time to time. These entities may be hospitals, pharmacies, or other organizations that provide healthcare. Each one maintains its own "version" of medication for that same patient. There is a likely chance that each entity's prescription might

differ slightly from that of other entities because each entity does not get to share their version of the medication. In some cases, this prescription medication may be electronic, but in cases of a duplicate paper prescription, these might be lost. Since blockchain technology is a system of a shared digital ledger, each medical entity, hospital, or pharmacy will see all the background information of that patient. When a pharmacy gets the prescription from a patient, they will now have all the information needed for that particular patient, his/her medical history and present condition, and will in no way question the doctor's prescription. They could also view past prescriptions and relate these to the current prescription. It will bring about a special kind of cohesion to the healthcare system made possible only because of the system's fidelity and accuracy.

2. **Improved Data Security for Patients**: Medical records are very confidential, and doctors respect this fact. They even take an oath before joining the medical profession. Blockchain technology will help doctors and caregivers at large maintain their integrity in this regard. They will be able to keep information for as long as they want and at the same time protect the identity and information of every single patient.
3. **Accuracy**: Information about medical records, past and present diagnosis, and history of a particular patient's medical condition will all be readily available (stored on a digital ledger), and these records remain unalterable.
4. **Specialized Data Sharing**: We remember that blockchain technology uses the concept of "smart contracts," which makes automated execution of milestones possible. Not only will data elements be distributed from a patient

to a healthcare giver or organizations, but instead of storing the actual data, it will also be encrypted, and only authorized personnel can decrypt it (provided with passwords) and access the information.

Relevance in Real Estate

Blockchain technology allows individuals or organizations to transfer information, money, or other types of assets quickly and without a need for intermediaries. It can also be used to easily transfer real estate. We will now examine three different ways blockchain technology will improve or totally transform real estate for the better.

- Prevention of Fraud
- Disintermediation
- Smart Contracts

Prevention of Fraud: In the world of transactions, fraud is a major problem. Everybody wants to make quick money, and they try all sorts of means, ranging from forging different kinds of data and paperwork to misrepresentation of bank invoices and statements, deeds, drivers licenses, all in a bid to make more money. Real estate fraud is also common, and the rate at which this crime has been increasing in recent times is alarming. Even the world's largest and most secure banks still fall victim to such criminal acts once in a while, but how can blockchain technology prevent these criminal acts in real estate? This is what Don Oparah, CEO of a London-based IT firm, has to say about how blockchain will improve real estate transactions: "By offering a 100 percent incorruptible resource, whereby a sender and recipient of funds was logged, and where digital ownership of certificates for properties are saved, the blockchain could effectively make forged ownership of documents and false listings a thing of the past. The unique digital ownership of certificates would be almost impossible to replicate and would be directly linked to one property in the system, making selling or advertising properties you do not own impossible. So it is clear that frauds in real estate transactions will be reduced to its barest minimum by blockchain technology."

Disintermediation: Real estate transactions can be complicated at times due to the presence of and need for third parties or intermediaries to complete the transactions. These third parties may include escrow companies, stockbrokers, inspectors, appraisers, or even government agencies in some cases. These transactions will be stalled for many days until the intermediaries complete their tasks, and it can cost money and waste valuable time. It is similar to when we depend on them to complete the deals. Why are middlemen needed in transactions related to real estate? Why do we need them to validate our title deeds and other documents? It is because they have skills and licenses that we don't have, and they have access to some information that we cannot access, and these licenses and information are needed for these transactions to be completed. As we already know about blockchain technology, it is a digital ledger that is made public, and access to everyone connected is granted at the same time without needing any form of permission or without any information being withheld. It means that every property will be able to handle transactions themselves anytime without the need for any third party.

Let us take TITLE as an example. The title to a property is currently just a piece of paper. The paper needs to be filled out correctly, signed with possibly a pen and the middleman, and a notary most likely puts a rubber stamp on it. It then goes to the county's recorder, who manually puts it in their database. Taking a look at the whole process, you will notice all the wasted time and money to record this information in the database. Blockchain technology can help make the process much simpler. It will replace a paper title, and a cryptocurrency (e.g., bitcoin) will be used to create a digital title. It can then be transferred easily over the Internet to the necessary agencies, nullifying the need for a third party and saving valuable time as well.

Smart Contracts: It seems that one of the best features of the blockchain is the smart contract. There will no longer be a case of a party fulfilling its obligations while the other party refuses. It is automated, as the contract will go on as long as certain mutually agreed-upon conditions are met. An example is that you will be paid as soon as you reach a certain number of the consumer base. There will be fewer court cases, as transparency will make fraud a thing of the past.

Application in Government Structure

Nearly all governments worldwide are faced with these three common challenges: transparency, corruption, and trust. This has made many governments start looking into exploring blockchain technology to help them improve their operations and at the same time tackle these challenges. A recent survey by IBM and EIU shows the following:

- Nine in ten governments wants to invest in blockchain so that they can better manage financial transactions.
- 14 percent of government structures are expected to implement blockchain in at least one arm of governance by the end of 2017.
- Seven in ten governments believe that blockchain's use in government will alter the field of contract management.

It is no surprise that various governments have been outspoken in canvassing support for this new innovation. Let us take a look at four different ways blockchain technology can benefit governments and help them improve their operations.

4 Ways That Blockchain Technology Can Help Governments

1. Transfer of Assets: Moving assets, be it money, property, or value from one place to another or from one person to another will be made easier. Bilateral trades between different governments will improve, and the process of direct payment of funds will speed up.
2. Ownership: Since the blockchain is known for its preservation of "chains" of events and records of physical assets, the ownership of property titles, lands (boundaries), and any other type of physical asset ownership issues will be done away with, thereby promoting good relations.
3. Identities: When e-identities are provided by the government to its citizens, using every other service will be easier, e.g., voting. The e-identity is quite similar to international passports, as an owner is eligible to participate in every other activity within the country.

With the help of blockchain technology, this will be made possible.

4. Verification: Events, proof of records, transactions, and licenses will be adequately verified with the technology. Unscrupulous activities will be curtailed, and identity theft will be minimized.

It is expected that governments should start exploring blockchain technology through its proof of concept and other processes. It is totally harmless—doing more good with little or no harm. They should create more awareness for it and put people in charge of developing it. They should commit to making it better suited for their circumstances. They should also encourage citizens to embrace this innovation, as it gives more freedom and can both maximize strength and reduce costs.

Blockchain in Governments

The United Kingdom: The United Kingdom is exploring this new technology in the management of grants. Controlling the distribution of grants has often been subject to corruption. Since all involved parties connected to blockchain have the same information at the same time, the distribution of grants will be better managed.

Estonia: Estonia has used blockchain technology to create the concept of e-residency. This program has allowed anyone anywhere in the world to be able to apply and become an e-resident of the country. This e-residency is not different from normal residency because an e-resident can use the same services available to a resident by birth. Estonia is also using this technology to improve its health sector, especially in managing medical records.

Ghana: This West African nation is looking to utilize this technology in managing property ownership because of corrupt individuals in positions of trust.

Sweden: This Scandinavian country wants to use blockchain technology in making real estate transactions more efficient. The feature of this innovation most useful to them is the elimination of intermediaries.

Singapore: The major reason this Asian nation is exploring blockchain is to curb the frequent cases of customers defrauding banks. Two years ago the country's standard chartered bank lost almost $200 million to fraud. Fraudsters in this country also occasionally duplicate bank invoices and get return money from banks.

Engineering Development in Poorer Countries

One thing that is synonymous with developing countries is a developing economy, and every developing economy wants to grow and achieve "developed" status. The blockchain network can help these developing countries facilitate the process of change from "developing" to "developed." The technology has been seen to have great potential for all who implement it. Developing nations are only making life harder for themselves, but with this technology, not only will they better their lot economically, but they will also find normal day-to-day operations easier. In developing nations, some rules govern transactions, but these rules are not implemented. So it happens that any service that depends on these types of rules does not take place. An instance is opening an account in most banks in Africa. These banks require prospective account holders to deposit a considerable minimum opening balance, which can be equivalent to a person's annual income, but here is how blockchain technology will help out in that regard: simple transaction rules are set that ensure authentication and not an opening balance. These rules will make banking both simple and affordable. That is just an example, as there are many other ways that blockchain technology will help bring about development in these poor lands.

1. **Sending Money Internationally**: Last year an estimated $442 billion was sent from individuals in developed lands to their families back home in poorer countries. We can't question this because they aim to make life better for them. All of us certainly want to help our families in need, but can you imagine the amount of money needed to transfer such a large amount of funds? We all know that money can be sent by MoneyGram, Western Union money transfer, and other such entities, and they charge for their services. Using digitalized blockchain technology for such transfers will result in bypassing

bank charges and the common remittance protocols. More funds will be saved and sent home.

2. **Helping Small Businesses**: It can be very hard for some businesses in these developing lands to apply for a loan and be approved because access to loans in these countries greatly depends on middlemen. Not only have these loans been hard to get, but they also attract very high interest rates. Banks also refuse to grant loans in areas well known for corruption and fraud. Blockchain technology will help nullify the role of these middlemen and will promote transparency, which will reduce fraud. Small businesses will be able get loans and extend their borders.

3. **Humanitarian Aid**: Sometimes, nongovernmental organizations and foreign companies in richer countries send money, clothes, and other forms of relief to these poorer countries, especially when disaster strikes. In some

cases, it turns out that this humanitarian assistance is not used for its intended purpose due to corruption and mismanagement. There is also the challenge of the cost of transporting relief material to these target countries. Blockchain can help in two major ways. It can reduce the cost of transportation and keep track of how this humanitarian aid is used. Donors can actually be confident that what they want done with their resources is respected and adhered to.

4. **Insurance**: Lack of access to basic amenities, such as healthcare and insurance in developing countries, is due to lack of income. The money required to have access to these amenities is more than what they make. Insurers also tend to exploit these low-income earners by siphoning money from them. This technology will ensure that these processes will be restricted to an online mode, which will reduce the corrupt

insurers' impact. It will also give customers the option of paying in smaller amounts.

Chapter 4: Future Use of Blockchain Technology

In the coming years, further applications of this technology may include:

- **Tracking Taxpayer Money**: Hancock, speaking at the Digital catapult headquarters in King's Cross said, "We are exploring the use of blockchain to manage the distribution of grants. Monitoring and controlling the use of grants is incredibly complex. A blockchain accessible to all parties involved might be a better way of solving the problem. Bitcoin proved that distributed ledger can be used to track currency at it is passed from one entity to another. Where else could we use that? Think about the student loan company tracking money all the way from the treasury to a student's bank account."
- **Online Voting**: Currently, no country has yet to adopt this process. Maybe they fear it might not be totally secure, but some have used blockchain technology to improve the electoral system due to its transparency. Remember that

in 2014 the Liberal Alliance political party in Denmark became the first major party to conduct an internal voting process using blockchain technology. Their success has led many experts to consider this technology as the future of our electoral system.
- **Cloud Storage**: We can also expect blockchain to be applied as cloud storage systems of data because of its decentralized nature. This technology can distribute information across many connected servers all at the same time while still maintaining privacy, with absolutely no chance for program hackers and attackers.
- **Smartcard Payments**: By the end of this year through the start of 2018, payment cards that are entirely contactless and can process transactions almost immediately are expected to hit the market. Today, merchants and dealers can utilize this as an alternative to payment services.
- **Expanded Digital Identity**: Industries lose an estimated $18.5 billion annually on improving digital security. Taking a closer look

at that figure shows that for every $3 spent $1 goes to protecting online identity. Blockchain's automatic tracking and digital management will solve these problems, which will be useful in almost every facet of identification, such as passports, e-residency, birth and wedding certificates, citizenship, healthcare, and licenses.

This technology can also be applied in many other ways. The legal system will improve as will land registration and every form of online payment and subscription. The list goes on. The bottom line is that blockchain is here to stay.

Conclusion

When we were children, we always depended on others for almost everything—support, food, and even simple tasks, such as sleeping. As we grow older, though, we learn to do some things on our own. In today's world, we can't expect to depend on people for everything, especially in the business world. This book has been expository regarding how blockchain can help you grow your business and other activities. The prospects are amazing. In ten years' time, I am sure that blockchain will be on the lips of everybody on this planet. It may even be taught in colleges. Many governments will have ministries dedicated to the development of blockchain technology. It will be in the news every hour, and every country will legalize it. Other fields will be affected as well. With its ever-growing possibilities, it might just be your ticket to hitting the jackpot. It is no longer a myth. It is reality and the new speed of economy. I hope to see you at the top.

— George Icahn

More Books By George Icahn

Check out my Author Central Page:
http://www.cryptocurrencystudio.com/george icahn

ETHEREUM

The Complete Guide To Understanding Ethereum

George Icahn

About this book
Introduction to Ethereum
Cryptocurrency Secrets + Newsletter
CHAPTER 1
- Understanding Ethereum
- Ethereum developers and its early days
- Early Days
- Progress Made So Far
- Ethereum's Timeline
- The Ethereum Foundation

CHAPTER 2
- Ethereum as a Cryptocurrency
- Transactions
- Ethereum's Blockchain
- Block Size
- Blockchain Size
- Block Times
- Ethereum's Consensus Algorithm
- Why Proof of Stake?

What would be the repercussions of the proof of stake on Ethereum price?
- Mining Ethereum
- The Ethereum Virtual Machine
- Solidity

Ethereum's Supporting Technologies
CHAPTER 3
Trading and Availability

The "Gas"

A Closer Look at the Market

Pricing

Market Movement

Global Adoption

Challenges Facing the Growth

PROFERRED SOLUTIONS

Development Timeline

Latest News On Ethereum

Conclusion

About this book

This book is about to expose you to the rather underrated digital currency known as Ethereum. If you are already interested in digital currency and blockchain technology, I am sure that you are familiar with the Bitcoin. Well, that is the first digital currency as you may already know. But, Ethereum has a very high potential to usurp the Bitcoin as the most popular and useful cryptocurrency in years to come because of the things you can do with it. As you go over this book, you will find out some interesting facts about it as well as how it can multitask cryptographically and economically. If you are interested in boosting your economic output, joining in making history and making a difference, then this book is for you.

Introduction to Ethereum

Ever since the introduction of the Bitcoin as a cryptocurrency, there have been many other digital currencies in the market. According to current statistics, there are some 900 types of cryptocurrency available right now, and much more are expected in years to come. Until recently, we all know that building an application that uses blockchain will require a complex coding background, cryptography, solving some mathematical problems and well as significant resources. But technology is advancing;

previously unimagined applications are now hitting the market. Electronic voting, digitally recorded property assets, digital regulatory compliance, and trading, to mention a few, are now being actively developed and are made available on an unprecedented scale more than ever before. Ethereum is that tool that is designed to provide developers the needed software to build various kinds of decentralized applications.

Is Ethereum similar to Bitcoin? Can we trade with it? How does it work? Many people have been asking me these questions. Well, let me tell you in the simplest of terms. Ethereum is not really like Bitcoin but sure shares some similarities. It is a distributed public blockchain network, just like the Bitcoin. But as per the technical differences, one major difference is that Bitcoin and Ethereum differ in purpose and capability.

Without dwelling too much on that, let me tell you that the purpose of this book is to give you all the information there is about Ethereum. You will appreciate the in-depth analysis as well as the comments of some experts making use of this software. I hope you enjoy the ride.

Cryptocurrency Secrets + Newsletter

Join my **FREE** Cryptocurrency Newsletter to start receiving more information related to everything FinTech. It will help keep you on track. You will also be notified about my new books (at a special discounted price).

The best part? When you subscribe, you will immediately receive my **"Cryptocurrency Secrets"** Report where you will discover exciting contents such as: _The type of cryptocurrencies available, strategies to invest, how to collect more bitcoin, and much more!_ It's just my way of saying thank you for your readership!

Follow The Link Below To Subscribe And Get Free Instant Access:

cryptocurrencystudio.com/offer

CHAPTER 1

Understanding Ethereum

The Ethereum blockchain's focus is on running the codes necessary for programming any decentralized application. We notice that it is different from the bitcoin blockchain that can be used to keep track of the ownership of digital currency. Bitcoin only offers a peer-to-peer electronic cash system that makes online Bitcoin payments possible. But in the Ethereum blockchain, miners do not mine for bitcoins, rather they work to earn "Ether", which is a crypto token that powers the network. It goes one step beyond a cryptocurrency that can only be used to trade by also being used by application developers to pay for the transaction fees incurred and other services in the Ethereum network.

All blockchains have the ability to process codes, not all can do it extensively. But the Ethereum stands out in that in that it is not limited to just some operations like other blockchains, it goes further by enabling developers to create any kind of operations they so ever desire. Developers can use Ethereum to create thousands of other different supplications that go way beyond anything we have seen before.

Ethereum also has one important feature associated with digital currencies, the smart contract. What is a smart contract? A contract that is smart, is that what you are thinking? Well, the smart contract is just a phrase used in describing computer codes that can facilitate the exchange of money, property, shares, contents and virtually anything that has value. In a blockchain network, the smart contract is a computer program that self-operates when certain conditions are met. The smart contracts run as exactly as they are programmed without any possibility of expurgation, downtime, and fraud or a third party interference. Don Tapscott, a Canadian business executive who specializes in business strategy, organizational technology and the role of technology in business has this to say about Ethereum:

"Ethereum blockchain has some extraordinary capabilities. One of them is that you can build smart contracts. It's kind of what it sounds like. It's a contract that self-executes and the contract handles the enforcement, the management, performance, and payment"

Some have termed Ethereum "the next internet".

That phrase is a phrase that's often used when discussing Bitcoin, the decentralized digital currency, and the blockchain, its distributed global ledger. Yet, the phrase is perhaps misleading in its simplicity. While commonly referred to as a singular construct, "the Internet" is rather a web of protocols and rule sets that combine to power complex communications, collaboration and business processes. When viewed similarly, "the blockchain", or the public, permission less blockchain protocols could be seen as a more primitive version of what could become a mature "Internet of Value". Such a public utility could one day provide a similarly layered architecture to expand the Internet of Information or the Internet as we know it today, to deliver all manner of financial and non-financial transactional services. If the Internet decentralized access to information, thereby increasing access to communication tools, the vision for the blockchain is that it would decentralize, and reduce barriers to establishing trust and transacting in the digital world. First introduced in 2014, Ethereum can be seen as both a realization of this future and recognition of the limitations of the bitcoin network, the first widely used public blockchain.

In his keynote announcement for the project, creator and inventor Vitalik Buterin described ethereum in such terms, arguing that Bitcoin was not designed to serve as the blockchain's answer to the Transmission Control Protocol (TCP) or Internet Protocol (IP), the code that forms the basic communication language of the internet. Buterin wrote: "Bitcoin was designed to be a [Simple Mail Transfer Protocol] SMTP. It's a protocol that is very good at one particular task. It is good for transferring money, but it was not designed as a foundational layer for any kind of protocols to be built on top." In remarks, Buterin spoke of the need for a technology that was more expansive, and that replicated the functionality of Turing-complete programming languages in a way that would be so powerful as to describe any blockchain application that could possibly be built.

He later added that: "Ethereum does not have features; it just has a programming language."

Ethereum developers and its early days

Ethereum was initially proposed sometimes during the fourth quarter of 2013 by Vitalik Buterin, a researcher whose research works are all about digital currencies. He is also a computer programmer. He announced that it is the result of his research work in the Bitcoin community. Sometimes afterward, he published the Ethereum white paper, where he described in detail the technical design and foundation for the Ethereum protocol and smart contract architecture. The development of Ethereum was funded by an online crowdsale between July and August of 2014. So, its release date is pegged at January 2014 because that was when Ethereum was formally announced by Vitalik at The North American Bitcoin Conference in Miami, Florida, USA. The Ethereum system went live on the 30th of July, 2015; with around 11.9 million coins already mined for crowdsale.

Shortly after then, Mr. Vitalik started working with Dr. Gavin Wood, a medical Doctor with years of experience as a renowned surgeon, and together, they co-founded Ethereum. Dr. Gavin published the Ethereum Yellow Paper that would later serve as the technical specification for the Ethereum Virtual Machine (EVM), in April 2014.

By following the detailed specification in the Yellow Paper published by Dr. Gavin, the Ethereum client has been implemented in seven programming languages namely C++, Go, Python, Java, JavaScript, Haskell, and Rust.

In 2016, The DAO (Decentralized Autonomous Organizations) project collapsed and as a result of that Erethreum was forked into two blockchains. The majority of the two being Ethereum.

Early Days

Ethereum was created with the aim of building software that will create numerous decentralized applications. Buterin had argued that Bitcoin needed a scripting language for application development. Failing to gain agreement, he proposed the development of a new platform with a more general scripting language.

Although he started the research alone, he was later joined by Dr. Gavin Wood who later became a co-founder of Ethereum. The original four members of the Ethereum team were Vitalik Buterin, Mihai Alisie, Anthony Di Iorio, and Charles Hoskinson. Formal development of the Ethereum software project began in early 2014 through a Swiss company, Ethereum Switzerland GmbH (*EthSuisse*). Eventually, a Swiss non-profit foundation, the Ethereum Foundation (*Stiftung Ethereum*) was set up as well. Development was funded by an online public crowdsale during July–August 2014, with the participants buying the Ethereum value token (ether) with another digital currency, bitcoin. While there was early praise for the technical innovations of Ethereum, questions were also raised about its security and scalability.

Several prototypes of the Ethereum platform were developed by the Ethereum Foundation, as part of their Proof-of-Concept series, prior to the official launch of the Frontier network. The last of these prototypes culminated in a public beta pre-release known as "Olympic". The Olympic network provided users with a bug bounty of 25,000 units of ether for stress testing the limits of the Ethereum blockchain.

After Olympic, the Ethereum Foundation announced the beginning of the Frontier network to mark the tentative experimental release of the Ethereum platform in July of 2015. Since the initial launch, Ethereum has undergone several planned protocol upgrades called milestones, which are important changes affecting the underlying functionality and/or incentive structures of the platform.

The current milestone is named "Homestead" and is considered stable. It includes improvements to transaction processing, gas pricing, and security. There are at least two other protocol upgrades planned in the future, i.e. Metropolis and Serenity. Metropolis is intended to reduce the complexity of the EVM and provide more flexibility for smart contract developers. The move to Serenity is still uncertain but should include a fundamental change to Ethereum's consensus algorithm to enable a basic transition from hardware mining (proof-of-work) to virtual mining (proof-of-stake). Improvements to scalability, specifical sharding, are also said to be a key objective on the development roadmap.

Progress Made So Far

Even though still in its early days, Ethereum has already seen a number of projects emerge that are seeking to bring its core concepts to life. Far from just theory, Ethereum-based projects are inspiring developers, overcoming challenges in the wild, inspiring research papers, grabbing global headlines and operating without the backing of a conventional corporate structure. Let us now discuss some early and notable examples.

The DAO (Decentralized Autonomous Organizations)

The most prominent ethereum project yet launched, The DAO was a DAO designed to collect ether investments and distribute those funds to projects voted on by an open community of donors and members. In its short lifespan, The DAO amassed upwards of $160m denominated in ether, and saw a number of proposals put forth for voting, though none were passed. The DAO quickly emerged as a magnet for academic criticism about how DAOs should be designed and their participants incentivized. At this time however, the project had effectively collapsed following an incident in which an attacker was able to exploit functionality in The DAO's code. Called a "recursive call exploit", the attacker effectively requested funds from The DAO repeatedly, and the contract approved these fund requests without first checking the balance. Presently, ethereum developers were considering a number of possible solutions to the loss of customer funds. These included a hard fork, or alterations to ethereum's code that would effectively reverse the hack, and a soft fork, which would enact code preventing the stolen funds from being redeemed. While live, approximately 10 million DAO tokens changed hands daily on the ethereum network.

Other DAOs

Currently, a number of smaller DAOs have raised funds in ether or are in early stages of development, and trends in the market were beginning to take shape. Digix, a DAO meant to create a gold-tracking asset for ethereum, raised $5.5 million in March in a crowdsale. MakerDAO, likewise, intends to launch a "stablecoin" with a fixed value that can enable a credit-based monetary system on the network. This formation, in which a team of developers raises money to deliver code that can then be managed by a diversity of participants, seems most common among entrepreneurs seeking to launch products or exchanges centered on ether trading or investing. Other notable projects that don't quite fit into this framework include Golem Project, which is building technology that would allow users to trade the idle time of their computers, and Augur, a decentralized prediction market.

Augur

Positioned as the first open-source, decentralized prediction market, Augur seeks to enable its global users to bet on the outcome of future events, with the goal of encouraging collective forecasting. The development team aims to use the decentralized nature of blockchains to avoid issues that have historically plagued predictions markets with centralized management seen as a point of failure that allowed earlier efforts to be shuttered by global governments. Augur is rare among ethereum projects as it intends to leverage multiple blockchain technologies as well as the Bitcoin currency to facilitate its operations and thus provides a compelling example of how future projects could leverage similar designs.

How Augur Uses the Ethereum Blockchain

Augur uses ethereum to remove the need for users to trust counterparties, reduce costs and make the platform resilient against central points of failure. The platform automates the custodianship of funds as well as the trading and settlement of these funds through smart contracts on ethereum, and by virtue of its design, allows all of it to be done with minimal trust.

How Augur Works

Augur requires a lot of ethereum calls. It's not uncommon for a user to automatically make hundreds of RPC calls; or messages sent between the user and ethereum nodes, during an instance of using Augur. These calls are "free", although they consume bandwidth and time. Let's take the following example:

An Augur user wants to bet that a Republican nomination for the US presidency will be named the party's nominee. On 11th April, the candidate had received 30% of the vote necessary for the nomination and ETH was valued at $15. A user would make a bet on this future outcome, paying $0.30 per share in ETH, that it will come to pass. If this user bought 1,000 contracts, and his nominee was victorious, he or she would receive a payout of $300.

How does this work?

Action 1: An Augur user will submit a bid or make an order. Orders are executed if another trader will match or offer better terms. Augur's middleware handles the various serialization, networking and formatting tasks required to communicate the order from the web application to Augur's ethereum smart contract, and sends a success/failure confirmation back to the user interface.

Action 2: The market reaches its end date. Augur users collectively report what happened to the blockchain using a "commit and reveal" encryption scheme that keeps reporters from knowing how others voted.

Action 3: Traders in possession of prediction market shares receive (or don't receive) automated payouts according to the outcome determined by Augur's reporting system. This functionality is facilitated through Augur's middleware and smart contract system on the ethereum blockchain.

Though still in its early stages, the first wave of ethereum projects is being observed with interest by venture capital firms with an expertise in the blockchain domain, with some receiving seed-level investments to develop more mature business strategies. While a positive indicator, it remains to be seen what role venture firms will play in the development of the ethereum startup ecosystem as a whole, given that the platform was meant to encourage the launch of communal projects incorporating the new governance structures its design and technology make possible. One early trend is that more traditional startups in the ecosystem are seeking to position their platforms as enablers of ethereum DAOs and decentralized projects either through ancillary services or specialized technologies. This differs from the historic rollout of the bitcoin network, as many startups sought to develop key infrastructure (exchanges and wallets) intended to be used directly by consumers. Here are some of the more notable companies to yet emerge:

- **Ethcore**

Where the headquarter is located: Mittweida, Germany
Venture Funding: $750k
Major Investors: Blockchain Capital, Fenbushi Capital
Number of Employees: 11-50

Led by ethereum's co-founder and former project CTO Gavin Wood, Ethcore develops software solutions for enterprise businesses and financial institutions that want to leverage the network's technology as well as the firm's subject expertise. The startup offers a premium ethereum client called Parity, which processes blocks on the network performing tasks including database population, EVM code execution, proof-of-work verification, receipt verification and transaction signature checking. It further intends to embark on the creation of application-level libraries for developers, while adding IoT features to its Parity roadmap.

Key Events:

JANUARY 2016 – Ethcore begins working with French bank BNP Paribas to explore use cases of blockchain technology.

APRIL 2016 – Ethcore releases version 1.0 of its Parity client, the first component of its blockchain technology suite.

- **Ether.camp**

Where the headquarters is located: New York, USA
Venture Funding: Undisclosed
Major Investors: Undisclosed
Number of Employees: 1-10

A company that grew out of ConsenSys' hub-and-spoke development model, Ether.camp primarily offers technology tools, including an integrated development environment that serves as a sandbox for developers. On the technology front, Ether.camp provides a studio for smart contract prototyping as well as a Java implementation of the ethereum protocol. Elsewhere, Ether.camp provides network transparency tools similar to that of Bitcoin industry startup, the Blockchain technology, enabling users to both gain insight into publicly available data about Ethereum and track contracts on the network.

Key Events:

OCTOBER 2015 – Ether.camp is among the first projects to have its technology made available in Microsoft Azure.

- **BlockApps**

Where the headquarter is located: New York, USA
Venture Funding: Undisclosed

Major Investors: Undisclosed
Number of Employees: 12

BlockApps aims to enable enterprise businesses to launch private, consortium or public blockchain applications through a full-stack blockchain infrastructure solution. The company's signature offerings are STRATO, a single-node blockchain instance that uses a RESTful API to serve as a developer sandbox for Ethereum applications, and Bloc, a web application software development kit that supports Ethereum smart contracts.

Key Events:

FEBRUARY 2016 – BlockApps is named the first public partner of open source tech giant Red Hat, joining its OpenShift Blockchain Initiative.

MARCH 2016 – BlockApps becomes the first "certified offering" on Microsoft's Blockchain-as-a-Service (BaaS) offering in its Azure cloud computing platform.

These are just a few examples as there are many more companies that are expected to emerge in the coming years.

Ethereum's Timeline

- JANUARY 2014 – Ethereum inventor Vitalik Buterin announces the project at The North American Bitcoin Conference.

- JULY 2014 – The Ethereum Foundation begins selling ether tokens in a 42-day public sale. In total, it sold 60,102,216 ETH for 31,591 BTC, worth $18,439,086 at that time.
- JULY 2015 – Ethereum launches Frontier, a command-line version of the platform for developer testing.
- AUGUST 2015 – Kraken becomes the first major digital currency exchange to list ethers for sale. Major exchanges including Coinbase and Gemini follow suit.
- JANUARY 2016 – Eleven major banks – Barclays, BMO Financial Group, Credit Suisse, Commonwealth Bank of Australia, HSBC, Natixis, Royal Bank of Scotland, TD Bank, UBS, UniCredit and Wells Fargo – announce a trial of a permissioned version of the platform.
- JANUARY 2016 – The first Ethereum startups begin to raise funding for projects as diverse as a decentralized stock market and developer tool suites.
- MARCH 2016 – Ethereum releases Homestead, the first "production-ready" version of its blockchain platform.
- MARCH 2016 – The total value of all ethers on the Ethereum network passes $1bn.

- MAY 2016 – The DAO becomes the largest decentralized autonomous organization, collecting more than $160m worth of ethers to be invested in other projects.
- JUNE 2016 – The DAO collapses after an unknown attacker exploits a flaw in the project's code. The event forces Ethereum's development community to consider protocol-level code changes to rescue customer funds

The Ethereum Foundation

The leading organization behind the Ethereum project is the Ethereum Foundation (Stiftung Ethereum), and it was established in June 2014 as a non-for Profit Company in Zug, Switzerland. Zug is a small city of 24,000 people, has made a concerted effort to help drive its local economy by taking a progressive stance toward such projects. The Ethereum Foundation is the entity which issued the initial ether sale, and it was created to oversee this process, manage to fund the development and pay back debt the effort had incurred through legal bills in the run-up to its launch. The non-profit has an ongoing effort to organize and coordinate the community, managing accounts on Meetup, YouTube, Twitter, Q&A forum Stack Exchange and Facebook. While the Ethereum Foundation has a very little actual formal influence on many of the projects in the space, there is a high degree of crossover between those who work at the Foundation and those involved in other prominent projects. Today, the Ethereum Foundation is led by a governing and an advisory board and special advisors, and is organized as follows:

Vitalik Buterin- the creator of Ethereum

Mr. Buterin co-founded Bitcoin Magazine in September 2011. Eventually moving on to development, he sold the platform and wrote the ethereum white paper in November 2013. He now leads ethereum's research team.

Jeffrey Wilcke- One of the founders of Ethereum

Mr. Wilcke started the first implementation of ethereum using the "Go" programming language in 2013 and was the Go team lead at the time of the release of the genesis block and ethereum platform.

David Ben Kay- A lawyer

Mr. David specialized in creating innovative intellectual property solutions for emerging markets in Asian markets; Kay was formerly the General Counsel of Microsoft China.

Ming Chan - The Executive Director

An alumni of Massachusetts Institute of Technology, has a background in enterprise IT and management consulting projects, founding and growing businesses, and working with top educators, scientists, and inventors to bring inspiring research innovation to life. Her work includes legal and regulatory matters related to blockchain technology

The Advisory Board Members

The advisory board members consist of Bernd Lapp, a former head of sales at German Mobile app Centralway; Stefano Bertolo, a scientific project officer at the European Commission and Yessin Schiegg, CFO of Zurich-based consulting firm Alpha Associates.

Other Special Advisors include entrepreneur and author William Mougayar; Thomas Greco, A special adviser to Asian FinTech company Omise; and Vladislav Martynov, CEO and co founder of Yota Devices.

Aside from developing the Ethereum software, the ability to launch a new digital currency and its blockchain sure requires a great deal of time and effort to start from the scratch. It is not an easy thing to start assembling the resources needed to get it up and running. Ethereum announced its plan to do a presale of ether tokens, the currency of Ethereum. This is in a bid to kickstart the large network of developers and miners as well as investors.

Legal entities like the Ethereum Foundation (earlier discussed) was established to help cater for the complex process of the legalities and funding associated with this project. In July 2014, ethereum distributed the initial allocation of ether tokens via a 42-day presale (will be discussed in detail later) that was made public; and it netted about 31,591 units of Bitcoins worth $18,439,086 USD at the time, in exchange for about 60,102,216 units of ether. The result of this presale was initially used to pay back mounting legal debts and also as compensation for the efforts of developers that was not yet rewarded at the time. The left-over funds was used to finance the ongoing development of Ethereum as a cryptocurrency.

Following the success recorded from the presale of ethereum, its development was now formalized under a non-profit organization called the ETH DEV. This new arrangement will later go on managing the development of ethereum under the tutelage of the Ethereum team made up of Vitalik Buterin, Gavin Wood, and Jeffery Wilcke. They serve as the three directors of the organization. Developer interest in ethereum grew throughout the release year, 2014; and the ETH DEV team delivered a series of proof of concept (PoC) releases for the development community to evaluate. Different posts by the ETH DE team on the ethereum blog also helped to keep the excitement and momentum around ethereum going.

Increasing traffic and growing user-base on both the ethereum forum and ethereum subreddit testified that the platform is attracting a fast growing and devoted developer community. That trend has continued down to this day and it is expected to keep improving.

CHAPTER 2

Ethereum as a Cryptocurrency

As we have seen earlier, Ethereum is a decentralized software platform that runs on smart contracts (quite similar to the bitcoin)- digital applications that auto-executes or that runs exactly as programmed as long as certain agreed conditions are met, and this happens without any third party help or any possibility of fraud, downtime or external control whatsoever. These kinds of applications are powered by a custom built Blockchain-a powerfully shared global, numerical or digital (online) ledger that records transactions that are made in cryptocurrencies, sequentially and openly. This Blockchain technology is capable of moving value around and representing ownership of assets.

This foundation allows the developers of Ethereum to create an online marketplace where funds are moved back and forth (maybe in compliance with a past record; like a will, or a future contract condition), store registries of debts or promises, perform all other transactions that we haven't heard of, even going a step ahead of the Bitcoin, all without any interference from a third party.

Just like the Bitcoin, Ethereum has its own network wallet. The Ethereum wallet allows you to hold and secure Ether- which is a crypto token that powers the network, and other crypto assets that are built on the Ethereum network. All these use the smart contracts synonymous with any digital currency. Just like any digital currency, you can Ether, which is the tradable digital token that can be used as a means of exchange or a representation of an asset. It can also be used as a proof of membership or a virtual share. The programmed ruleset always determines the number of tokens in circulation at any given time.

With the Ethereum, you can also create a contract that will hold a contributor's money until any set date- maybe until a business goal is reached (remember it uses smart contracts). The money will either be released to the project contractors or safely returned to you, depending on the outcome. You also have the option of using the token you created to keep track of the distribution of rewards (like any other cryptocurrency).

The Ethereum network can do more! If you have developed a business idea and have secured funds but you don't know how to go about hiring Managers, CFOs, CEOs, and people to do all your necessary paperwork; then the Ethereum network can help you. Isn't that amazing? Leave all the work to an Ethereum contract. It will help you collect proposals and submit them on your behalf using a totally transparent voting system. But you may ask, is that not like leaving my business for a machine or robot to handle? But, is that not better than outside influences and the possibility of a business crash? Your organization will be immune to any tamper from outside, corruption or fraud, as it will only carry out what it has been programmed to do. Remember that the Ethereum network is decentralized, meaning you will be able to render services with 100 percent guarantee.

In the preceding chapter, we did liken Ethereum to the internet. This is because Ethereum isn't made up of just one part. It is a non-exhaustive list of components that includes a cryptographic token and address system, a network of miners, a consensus algorithm, a blockchain ledger, the Ethereum Virtual Machine, a set of programming languages and complex economic structures. We are going to touch on these key components briefly and illuminate the functionality each provides to the larger ethereum network to give you an idea of how it really works. In discussing these components, take note that we will be comparing it with Bitcoin (with the feeling that you have already heard about it), for a better understanding.

In computer science, a scripting language is a programming language that supports scripts or programs designed for run-time environments that execute tasks and reduce the need for human operators. Because of this, scripting languages tend to be best utilized for experiments and rapid prototyping. Bitcoin has an intentionally rudimentary scripting language, and there's a reason for this. From its inception, bitcoin's developers have prioritized the ability to "push" transfers of Bitcoin via the Bitcoin network over all other applications. While there have been discussions about adding a more powerful scripting language to facilitate easier application development, the view of the Bitcoin development community has largely been that it is more important to prioritize censorship resistance and network security over adding functionalities to the code. Ethereum, by contrast, aims to be "Turing-complete." This means that, if a system has unlimited resources, memory, computational power and storage, then infinite "loops" can be executed. In other words, the logic and functionality that may be embedded in ethereum transactions are only practically limited by the availability of the protocol's native currency, However, this functionality comes at the cost of security. Powerful scripting allows for greater function, but the additional tools also create new potential attack vectors (We will discuss this later).

Transactions

The most notable difference between the two blockchains is that ethereum blocks contain both a transaction list and the most recent "state" of the ledger of these transactions. This is a necessary feature to manage two types of accounts:

Externally owned accounts (EOAs) - Defined as the basic form of account, EOAs interact with and generate updates on the ethereum blockchain.

Contracts- Contracts programmatically execute when they receive instructions in the form of a transaction from an EOA. Contracts can push or pull funds, and request these actions from other contracts, calling on the code to perform dynamic actions. Ethereum notably does not use transaction inputs or outputs, which deviates from the unspent transaction outputs (UTXO) model Bitcoin popularized. In Bitcoin's model, each newly minted Bitcoin becomes an unspent transaction output with an owner who retains the right to consume that Bitcoin at a later time. During a Bitcoin transaction, these UTXOs become the inputs that are "consumed" in the transaction. When these bitcoins are spent, or pushed, to another user, a brand new UTXO is created. Ethereum, by contrast, uses a more familiar method. It stores the current "state" of its network, including a full list of accounts and their associated balances. Rather than confirming that UTXOs used in a transaction are valid, ethereum determines whether the sender has a sufficient balance, much like a bank verifying whether a check will clear. This design feature becomes important when transactions include contracts as recipients. If the transaction recipient is a contract, then that contract's code will execute, changing both the state of that contract and potentially triggering other contracts to execute code as well.

Ethereum's Blockchain

Both Ethereum and Bitcoin operate global transaction ledgers that today achieve remote and distributed validation through the use of a Proof-of-Work (PoW) protocol, a design in which participants expend significant energy to identify unique pieces of data that can then be easily verified by the wider network. This data is used to generate blocks, or certain finite quantities of transaction data, which serve as a reference for all other network participants. The resulting blockchain is able to provide a history of the network at each of these intervals, creating a shared truth as it relates to events. Blocks in both Bitcoin and ethereum are today similar, containing information such as the block number (denoting how many blocks have passed since the initial block) and the difficulty (a metric that denotes how challenging it is to complete the work needed to create a block). On the Bitcoin network, the transaction script is "stateless", meaning there is no state prior to execution of the script, and an update to this state is not saved after its execution. Contracts on ethereum are considered "stateful", meaning that they are aware of past information stored on the network and, if instructed via smart contract, can be programmed to take actions in the future. When peers, or members of the ethereum network, receive a block of data, they then run all transactions to verify a mathematical figure representing the system state at that time. If the nodes can validate this data, they accept the block for inclusion on the blockchain.

Block Size

On the Bitcoin blockchain, blocks are limited in size to 1 MB. This not only creates a cap on a number of transactions that can be processed per second (currently it's seven), but it also has turned into a major point of contention within the bitcoin community as it seeks to increase this limit. Ethereum has no such limit on the size of its blocks. Because ethereum executes scripts and contracts, this is a necessity, as limiting the size of a block would not only stunt the concept of Turing-completeness but limit the amount of storage a contract could use to execute. Rather than limit the size of its blocks, ethereum employs a mechanism which makes contracts more and more expensive to execute the larger they are in size.

Blockchain Size

As on the Bitcoin network, the more transactions that are executed on ethereum, the more information all the peers on the network need to store. The need to track and store all these transactions, in turn, requires resources from the network of computers running the blockchain. As of May 2016, the size of the ethereum blockchain has grown to approximately 17 GB. While this is still dwarfed by the bitcoin network's blockchain size, which stood at a little under 69 GB that time, it's worth pointing out that the bitcoin network is over eight years old, while at 17 GB, ethereum has been operating for just nine months. At an average growth rate of around 1 GB per month, ethereum's blockchain is growing more slowly than Bitcoin's, which is expanding in size at approximately 3 GB per month. However, ethereum has gained significant traction since its genesis block, and as the network becomes more popular, that monthly growth rate could accelerate. While this could become a cause for concern, ethereum is currently seeking to migrate to a new consensus algorithm that aims to alleviate this issue.

Block Times

During its design phase, the ethereum team was also keen to address what they perceived as issues or limitations in the operation of the Bitcoin blockchain. One issue that attracted attention was the time it takes transactions on the network to settle against the blockchain. Bitcoin's blockchain adds new blocks roughly every 10 minutes, which means that a transaction is generally not confirmed on the ledger until this time. In practice, actual confirmations may take longer, as those who use the protocol generally wait for six confirmations, or six blocks, before considering a transaction settled. Bitcoin and ethereum are not the only blockchains, or ledger structures, that use consensus methods. Various protocols have various block times. The Ripple protocol, developed by San Francisco startup Ripple, is designed to update its state every three to six seconds. Ethereum has set its target on 12-second block times, though current block times are closer to 14 seconds.

Ethereum's Consensus Algorithm

For any distributed computing system to properly function there needs to be a mechanism by which the entire network can come to an agreement on its state, or how its token supply is divided among registered addresses on the network. Bitcoin uses what is referred to as "Nakamoto consensus". Truly the pivotal innovation behind Bitcoin, Nakamoto's invention solved a long-standing computer science problem known as Byzantine Fault Tolerance, or the Byzantine Generals' Problem, the idea that one cannot trust someone who has the potential motivation to lie, and one cannot trust the integrity of a given communication if it has first passed through an intermediary. Bitcoin solves this problem by creating a chain of proof of work. The miners on the blockchain expend energy to solve a complicated mathematical equation in a bid to receive rewards when they find the next "block". Since the next block always follows from the previous block (meaning you start the equation from the point of the block), miners rush to verify that the block is valid so they can quickly turn to finding the next block and claim the reward. It is the incentive compatibility, and also immutable nature of entries in the blockchain, that provides a solution to the Byzantine Generals' problem. Although there are plans in the future to migrate the network to a different protocol in the years ahead, at the time of writing, ethereum uses a similar Proof of Work protocol known as Ethash. Ethash differs from Bitcoin's "Nakamoto-style" algorithm in a number of ways, the most familiar of which is that it uses different cryptographic primitive for its hashing function, known as SHA-3, rather than SHA-256. While the differences are nuanced, Ethash is designed to make ethereum both resistant to the high-powered mining chips that currently dominate the bitcoin industry, and more accessible to "light" client implementations that allow users to use ethereum without needing to first download the ethereum blockchain to their device. This consensus algorithm uses the proof of stake to function properly.

How exactly does the proof of stake (PoS) work?

Proof of stake, basically means you need a (STAKE) to be able to mine or generate interest.
Proof of stake is same in economics like giving your money to the bank for safe keeping and they give you an interest each year.

Proof of stake works similar - So in order for you to earn more coins with a proof of stake implementation you will need to buy a stack of coins first, You will then notice that the longer you keep the coins in your wallet, you will start making new coins

There are two key motivations for the move to Proof of Stake:

Ethereum developers and researchers believe that consensus algorithms based on Proof of Stake (PoS) can provide a higher degree of security for a given amount of resource expenditure, compared with Proof of Work (PoW) consensus algorithms.

Ethereum developers and researchers believe that a new design called Casper resolves the important remaining issues with the current "state of the art" in Proof of Stake design. These issues include imperfect decentralization and vulnerability to certain types of attacks, as well as other economic and performance considerations.

Both topics touch on issues worth elaborating in their own questions and answers, so I'll be linking to other questions as I summarize the main reasons for these two motivations.

> The fundamental flaw of Proof of Work (PoW) is that the costs of attacking the system are equal to what is spent to run the system. High security thus can only be achieved at high operating costs. The idea is that the honest participants just outspend the dishonest.
> This is already today highly inefficient, but it does work for Bitcoin. As soon as the block subsidiary starts reaching zero, the ratio between the Market Capitalization and the costs of attacking Bitcoin becomes critical.

Why Proof of Stake?

- Costs: Proof of Stake (PoS) promises to solve this problem. An honest validator is expected to have very low costs, compared to the costs an attacker would incur.
- Less Censorship: Another problem Casper tries to solve is to disincentivize censorship. The PoW scheme of Bitcoin is, more or less, a zero-sum game. This means, if a miner loses a block (it does not get included in the main chain/ it gets censored), all other miners benefit from their loss. PoS for Ethereum will not be a zero-sum game but instead a coordination game, where the rewards for everyone are highest if every participant can include their blocks.
- Scalability: Finally, some scalability problems can be addressed more easily with PoS.

Why would Proof of Stake provide more security for a given investment of resources than Proof of Work?

First, some background is useful. The goal of a consensus algorithm in a public blockchain network is to let many different users agree on the current state of the blockchain even though they don't trust each other or any central authority. This is a challenging problem, and until the Bitcoin network first solved it in 2008 by using Proof of Work (a.k.a. "mining", a.k.a. "hashing") no really good solutions were known. So the "performance" of the algorithm wasn't originally that important--the fact that it could be done at all was impressive enough.

After Bitcoin showed that a solution to public consensus was possible, new ideas such as "Proof of Stake" began to pop up in its wake. Once new algorithms were proposed, the question turned from "does it work?" to "does A work better than B?"

There are several different ways to answer this question. One way to gain an insight into the potential promise of PoS protocols is to consider four factors in particular:

- The cost to cooperating "honest nodes" in the absence of hostile attack
- The cost to cooperating "honest nodes" during a hostile attack
- The cost to attacking "hostile nodes" if their attack is unsuccessful
- The cost to attacking "hostile nodes" if their attack is successful

By comparing these costs to block rewards and other potential gains we can estimate the amount of "honest node" resources required to both run the network and hold off an attacker of a given scale. This provides a reasonably fair way to compare the level of security provided by two different consensus protocols.

Another question: Which is a better digital currency model and why; proof-of-stake or proof-of-work? **PoW for a limited time**

This will make a huge crowd turn up, as it would result in a short term massive increase in people getting the coin, as they would take it like an investment that will be expensive later on as the coins are limited

PoS for years to come

With PoS to make sure people do not just dump, it is good to have a high staking rate otherwise they will not find it worth it, and your coin will just die. If you make the PoS rate too high people will just keep it and well the volume goes down, the rate goes a bit down and it doesn't really work out.

A good model could be 50% all the time or have a time-based model where the percentage decreases over time, such as 100% for first 3 months, 70% for next -- months, etc. This will make sure people hold the coin, but people not interested in long term investing will not keep the coin, and only people who think the coin is rare and has a good staking rate will keep it.

What would be the repercussions of the proof of stake on Ethereum price?

There are different paradigms of authentication of the validity of transactions, used to build consensus and ensure that the chain of blocks is normal. They are:
• Proof-of-work (PoW), or proof of work (used for bitcoin mining);
• Proof-of-stake (PoS), or proof of participation;
• Zero-knowledge-proof or minimally disclosed proof.
Proof-of-stake has been compared to "virtual mining" or "consensus by bet" because bonded validators make transactions called "bets" that provide them profit in some histories at the expense of a loss in other histories.
The crux of PoS is to get players in the Ethereum ecosystem to play by the rules without the need for miners. According to Vitalik Buterin and other Ethereum developers, the transition will create a more democratic model of governance by leveling the playing field of miners from a select few to a more distributed and decentralized pool of miners/validators. The gradual move to PoS will occur through a hard fork. However, the decision to

decrease the miner block reward and by how much can be voted on by members of the community.

Implementing PoS is no small feat, nor is the move without its own debate, but the important takeaway is that, unlike Bitcoin, Ethereum developers have been corresponding productively with the community at large in order to gauge public sentiment over the governance details of the Ethereum blockchain. By removing traditional mining from its consensus protocol, which has become an oligopoly of GPU farms, Ethereum is proactively designing a paradigm to avoid the problems Bitcoin is having while also reducing the network's reliance on the energy associated with mining as a whole.

The transition to PoS may also serve as an example to the entire blockchain space by offering a functioning alternative to achieving network consensus while reducing hardware and energy costs, as well as creating a framework for blockchain governance that is in line with decentralization.

Furthermore, PoS brings with it other developments such as "sharding" that, according to developers, will greatly advance the Ethereum platform further and inspire innovation for commercial use and mainstream adoption.

Mining Ethereum

Ethereum also differs from Bitcoin in its transaction validation, both as it stands today, and as the network intends to function as it implements key changes in the future. In 2009, the first Bitcoin users were able to run mining software on home computers, using CPU power. As bitcoins became more valuable, a race for hashing power began, leading innovators to develop more and more powerful mining equipment. Today, the majority of bitcoin mining is done in data centers, largely by VC-backed companies that control the production cycle of equipment and collaborative collections of individual miners known as mining pools. To mitigate this consolidation, ethereum mining was set up so that it could only be conducted with graphics processing units (GPUs). The network is permissionless, meaning that anyone who purchases a graphics card and elects to run an ethereum client can begin processing transactions. However, if the intended switch to a new "proof-of- stake" consensus protocol is completed – mining may no longer be needed in the near future.

The Ethereum Virtual Machine

The ethereum protocol is designed to do far more than process peer-to-peer transactions. It is designed to execute complex code, where the functionality is only limited by the imagination of its developers and available resources.

As such, a system is needed to interpret instructions, and on ethereum, this task is handled by ethereum virtual machines (EVMs). Smart contracts are facilitated and enforced through EVMs, which implement and execute instructions written in any of a variety of languages via a bytecode. A bytecode, also called a portable code, is a type of instruction set created to be executed by a software interpreter. Just like the example of an "if-then" argument in a Microsoft Excel spreadsheet (albeit with often much greater degrees of complexity), EVMs interpret the bytecode, evaluate the transaction states and execute the code to deliver predictable outcomes. Ethereum Virtual Machines, in particular deliver this through a "Turing-complete" scripting language – allowing at least in theory, for infinitely complex contracts.

Solidity

Ethereum would be incomplete without a native programming language – and that language is Solidity. Solidity is the code that makes it possible to run contracts or programs in a distributed manner. To describe Solidity crudely, it closely resembles the browser-based JavaScript language, but for executing ethereum contracts. In contrast to an "object-oriented" language like JavaScript (which combines variables, functions, and data to run certain human-operated commands), Solidity is "contract-oriented". It's run-time environment tasks are automated, and its objects are bundled together to avoid the need for manual commands. Solidity is often described as ethereum's scripting language, but it is actually a compiled language, not a scripting language. It compiles instructions into bytecode so that they can then be read by the network.

This is a critical feature given that contracts are not wholly complied and independent programs, but rather partially compiled programs that depend on EVMs to run. Solidity is also designed to express agreements that encode relationships and arguments that exist in real life. It, therefore, includes more concepts than an object-oriented language. Identity, ownership, and protections form a core part of the programming grammar, which doesn't have a parallel in JavaScript.

As the language matures and adds more libraries and users, it has the potential to create massive and powerful constructs that could end up having real-world applications. For example, the Internet of Things (IoT), the vision for connecting devices and appliances to the Internet, will require a massive amount of machine- to-machine communication, infrastructure, and contract execution. A language like Solidity could play a key role in enabling these devices to talk to one another.

Ethereum's Supporting Technologies

In addition to the main ethereum blockchain protocol, there are also supporting technologies in development that seek to help the network, and components built on the network, run more efficiently. For example, whole new protocols are being constructed that aim to increase the functionality of distributed applications, while tools are evolving to allow these programs to harness data from multiple blockchains.

While there may be little that unites the following concepts on the surface, all are aimed at making ethereum more flexible for developers and users.

Whisper

A communications protocol and tool set that allows applications built on the ethereum protocol to talk to each other; Whisper combines aspects of a distributed hash table and a point-to-point communications system. Whisper is best explained in practice as it can be used to help facilitate exchange by recording buy or sell offers, allow for the creation of general chat room-like apps or even provide "dark" communications between parties who don't know anything about each other.

With Whisper, you can imagine an ethereum application for whistleblowers who want to communicate to a journalist where they've stored a trove of data, but don't want their identity to be linked to that data.

Swarm

Swarm is a peer-to-peer file sharing system designed to efficiently store and retrieve data needed for use in ethereum applications and contracts. The easiest analogy to draw would be that Swarm is essentially BitTorren for ethereum.

As we will discuss later, storing data directly on the ethereum blockchain is expensive. While contract code will have to be stored on the chain, reference data needed for contract execution should not. For instance, if a simple contract were to say deliver an e-card with pictures, the photos would take up a lot of space. Perhaps a school would want to send out an album with photos of its latest graduating class. Such an application, if run on ethereum, might require a contract that is 1 KB, but is designed to deliver 1 GB of data. Storing and transacting that 1 KB of code might cost users a few cents, whereas storing the album itself could cost more. By instead storing the album remotely, and accessing the file via a BitTorrent-like system, this would allow ethereum applications to deliver the instructions, with the files to be transferred via Swarm, not the ethereum blockchain directly.

For smart contracts to execute properly, they need not just be a well-designed series of "if then" statements – they also need to know how to ascertain the accuracy of given inputs to those "if-then statements". If it's raining in New York City, and there are multiple reliable sources that can confirm it is raining, how does ethereum weed through potentially fraudulent sources to identify the veracity of the input? Here, there is a need for a construct that communicates outside realities to smart contracts. In ethereum, these are called 'oracles'. While a number of projects are building their own private Oracle systems [like the "Augur"], there have been some attempts to create platform-agnostic systems for verifying inputs to multiple blockchains. Though there are currently a limited number of data sources that can be cryptographically proven – it isn't hard to imagine a future in which smart technologies and the Internet of Things could allow all sorts of external data to be incorporated into contracts.

Mist

If ethereum is to be the new TCP/IP, the project needed a new version of 'browser', a usable frontend technology with which users explore the applications and offerings that utilize ethereum. Styled as a decentralized application discovery tool, Mist is meant to serve as a wallet for smart contracts that features a graphical interface and allows users to dynamically set transaction fees and manage custom tokens. Presently, Mist is still in beta and is under heavy development.

CHAPTER 3

Trading and Availability

You may be thinking that Ethereum works just like the Bitcoin in trading, but you might find it surprising that it is not designed that way. It is not designed to function like another globally accepted cryptocurrency. Instead, it is designed to pay for specific actions on the Ethereum network, with users earning "Ether" as a reward for using their computing power to confirm transactions and deals and acting as a reward for the user's contribution to the overall development of the Ethereum network. One important component of the ethereum network and one that has attracted the interest of investors is ether (ETH). ETH is a unit of account and store of value on the ethereum blockchain, equivalent to bitcoins (BTC) on the Bitcoin network. Ether, while having an economic value as a scarce commodity, is not meant to serve as an alternative currency like bitcoin. Rather, it has been positioned as a system resource that powers the creations of those seeking to use the platform. If Bitcoin's value is derived from the security of the network and its scarcity, ether has value because it is needed to execute scripts and contracts on the ethereum network. For that reason, ether has been called the "digital oil" to bitcoin's "digital gold".

But that does not mean that Ethereum network is somewhat substandard in the market. In fact, it is currently supported by many of the same exchanges and infrastructure that has built around Bitcoin all the while. For instance, the same platforms that sold other digital currencies like the bitcoin are also the same platforms that sell Ether. So, customers who bought units of Bitcoin- BTC, from platforms such as Bitfinex and Kraken can go to these websites to buy Ether- ETH also. One major difference is the development of Bitcoin market and the development of the Ethereum network. With bitcoin, users were able to process transactions on the network from the comfort of their homes using a home computer, and later on, home mining equipment like mining hardware. So as the number of participants increased progressively, the value of Bitcoin grows simultaneously. But the development of Ethereum did not take the same path because the circumstances surrounding its growth it is totally different from the circumstances surrounding the growth of Bitcoin.

When Ethereum was launched, the idea was all new. But in a bid to galvanize a global development of this idea, Ethereum launched a pre-sale of ether tokens. All these happened in 2014. This attempt worked as over $14 million was raised in what has been later referred to as a crowdfunding effort. Only that it looked similar to a kind of informal initial public offering (IPO). The funds or donations collected from this crowdfunding effort became the driving force behind the initial supply and the rate of insurance that existed later. For the role, they played in this crowd funding, contributors received about 60 million ether. 12 million ethers went to the development fund; with the majority of these 12 million ethers going to the wallets of Ethereum's early developers and contributors. The remainder of the amount of ether went to the non-profit Ethereum foundation, which was based in the Switzerland.

This amount of Ethers added up to an earlier supply of 72 million ETH. After these series of events, ethereum's protocol allowed the creation of 5 ETH for every completed block. This protocol allowed the coming into existence approximately 18 million ETH every year. Comparing it with bitcoin, you will notice that Bitcoin's supply rate is more consistent. This is because, in every 10 minutes, new tokens of roughly 25 BTC are added. This fast supply rate is due to the presence of hard-coded rules in the software that made it clear right from the outset that there will only ever be 21 million bitcoins. And this rule does not seem to be changing anytime soon.

The ethereum network includes a mechanism for releasing new ethers into the system over time. Of note for investors familiar with Bitcoin and other digital currencies, is that there is a difference of approach in ethereum. For example, in Bitcoin, the limit of all bitcoins that will ever exist is currently set at 21m BTC. Ethereum, by comparison, has no hard limit on how much of its token will exist in the future.

Rather, its development team sought to use its token system in a way that would encourage access by introducing 18m ethers per year through mining. This steady rate of inflation, they reasoned, would then decrease over time as the overall token supply increased. Developer Joseph Lubin wrote in his introduction of the issuance model that "New participants in the system will be able to purchase new ETH or mine for new ETH whether they are living in the year 2015 or 2115,"

So, in the ether market, much consistency is not guaranteed, unlike the Bitcoin market. During its launch in 2014, it was announced that ether's rule will soon change during the start of this year, but the consensus algorithm that will make this possible is still being developed.

Still, ether was created for more than executing transactions. While Bitcoin had succeeded in proliferating naturally over time through mining, the ethereum community sought to find a way to jumpstart this process and encourage a base of enthusiasts who could help the network grow. To reach a critical mass of developers, ethereum's team used ether as an incentivization method to bring the project to life. In July 2014, ethers became directly available for purchase on Ethereum.org, and more than $18m was raised through the effort. A point of contention that has emerged, centers on the legality of the initial sale. As of now, no action has been taken against any of the individuals or groups involved; nor has any action been taken against other blockchain development teams that have used this approach to community building. Nonetheless, the legal complexities involved have been acknowledged by its developers. As stated above, this issue is by no means unique to ethereum given that a finite piece of data that can be exchanged via a blockchain has no natural legal equivalent or definition. While global regulators have sought to label all cryptographic, blockchain-based tokens "virtual currencies", the term doesn't quite capture how innovators in the ecosystem perhaps want their technology to be used or understood.

The "Gas"

If ether served as a way to enable access to ethereum's world computer and ensure its functionality, an economic structure was also needed to limit access. In order to complement ether and better explain its function of its token, ethereum introduced the concept of "Gas," a throttling mechanism that determines, in real time, how much ether each contract costs. Gas has a fixed value, currently set at 10 "szabo", with one ether being made up of 1m szabo. The longer it takes for the contract to run, and the more systematic resources it requires, the more fuel is needed to execute the contract. Running contracts based on the Gas throttle, or ether limit, is a market-based solution that simultaneously limits the potential for hackers to spam the network and eliminates the need to set a fixed size for new transaction blocks.

A Closer Look at the Market

So in reality, what does the Ethereum market look like? Remember that Ethereum is more of a public utility, which makes it important to do a data analysis of the markets so it will strengthen our confidence in this digital means of exchange. Let us quickly look at the some of the current projects on the network; the observed development of the marketplace and the progress made so far.

Pricing

While there may be no true value of any digital asset, the ethereum market provides clarity as to what users and traders believe is the value of ether, a metric that could also be argued is indicative of overall confidence in the project. As an investment, ether has shown similar growth as Bitcoin the digital currency. At the time of ethereum's initial crowdsale, users were able to purchase 2,000 ETH with 1 BTC, which was trading for just over $600 at the time.

ETH has since seen its price rise and fall. Of particular note is that speculators seem to be attracted to coordinating action around major project releases.

Still, such downward movements have been slight compared to ETH's overall price appreciation. At the time of the crowdsale, the price of 1 ETH was roughly $0.30. Compared to its value of $16.30 currently, this represents a 4,666% increase in value. As the above graph shows, enthusiasm for ether is reflected in its recent price, and it has arguably been on an upward trajectory.

Market Movement

An in-depth analysis of the network's blockchain shows that trading is today driving the majority of volume, though how much could be defined as speculative is uncertain. Data from current Research shows approximately 750,000 ETH (about $10.8m at then prices) was being traded on digital currency exchanges daily in May, with this activity representing 50% of daily ether transactions. This figure has since increased to 5.8m ETH (or $81.2m), with this activity representing 66% of daily ether transactions. A deep dive into the data from blocks 1,468,000 to 1,568,000 on the ethereum blockchain shows which entities are the most active in transacting ether. During this observation period, 699,900 transactions (representing 14m ETH) took place. In total, 14% of these transactions were conducted on exchanges. By comparison, transactions sent between contracts (including those that are part of decentralized applications) accounted for 6.39% of the transaction total and 12% of volume. The remainder was conducted by mining pools and other unknown entities. The data shows that trading is still the dominant use of ether, and that decentralized applications, while beginning to come online, still account for only a small part of the network's activity today.

Global Adoption

Beyond the speculative use of Ethereum's token, there are metrics that suggest the platform is being adopted by an increasing number of application creators and users. The number of Ethereum transactions, for example, has been steadily rising, hitting roughly 45,000 transactions per day as of June 2017.

Overall, transaction figures have roughly doubled since January of the same year, even while the volume remains more inconsistent and closely tied to intervals of high price volatility.

Other positive indicators include the rising number of unique addresses and the increasing network difficulty, which indicate more users are joining the network and more miners are securing the network. Perhaps one of the strongest indicators of support for the ethereum network is the number of computers running versions of the ethereum client and its full blockchain history.

As of July 2017, ethereum had 5,384 nodes connected to its network, a figure that was just shy of the 5,757 observed on the older Bitcoin network. There is also an observable relationship between the geographical distribution of both networks, with the majority of nodes being hosted in the US and Germany.

Challenges Facing the Growth

While the work that has been done to date is without a doubt impressive, there is still much to be done to improve ethereum.

Let us now review some of the planned improvements and larger challenges facing the network's development team ahead of this goal.

The Scripting

Ethereum's programming language has been, and still remains a work in progress. Solidity is a brand-new concept in computer programing, and script-based systems remain largely untested. Further, the language's compiler is buggy, and there aren't repositories and public libraries yet. This makes creating functional smart contracts on ethereum difficult. Each module has to be as perfectly crafted as each gear in a Rolex. If the modules don't interact exactly as designed, the system breaks down. One independent review of the ethereum code exposed the extent of what is becoming a more widely acknowledged problem outside the network's development community, estimating are potentially 100 bugs per 1,000 lines of code. Compare that to Microsoft's one bug per 2,000 lines of code, and you have an idea of the extent to which the project may need to make improvements long term. While not all contracts will be as buggy as the one that was reviewed, the state of the solidity compiler is something that will need to be addressed before ethereum can scale. Imagine gears in a Rolex only working right with each other 90% of the time. You will spend a lot of time readjusting the time as it slipped out of sync. Such an issue could develop with ethereum's smart contract modules, except they may not just fail to keep proper time; they may stop working, suffer from security issues or potentially execute improper contract outcomes.

The Price of Gas

The economics of the platform is also in early stages. A lot of experts have argued that the price of gas is just too high. For instance, it cost $250,000 to process 1 GB of ethereum transaction data in May. At that time, the contract would cost 640,000,000,000 gas, or about 17,500 ETH, at $14 per ETH. To be fair, most contracts will be far smaller than

1 GB, and users would likely not want to store 1 GB of reference data on the ethereum blockchain when they could use a protocol like Swarm Hash. But storage and resources are still very expensive.

Mining Centralization

As discussed above, ethereum also sought to implement an architecture that would alleviate issues that have contributed to the centralization of mining power on the bitcoin network, enabling a wider variety of users to be incentivized to boost the platform as a whole. As recently as March 2016, however, one mining entity, dwarfpool, had amassed 48% of the network's hashrate, leading to concerns about centralization and the possibility that one entity could gain control of the network.

Such an attack would find the entity changing the ethereum ledger at will and forcing its version of the blockchain to be considered valid, thereby undermining trust in the network. A look at the network shows that its transaction validators have consolidated into a small number of entities and pools. However, this is due to the functionality of its existing PoW [Proof-of-work] protocol, which as we covered previously, is designed to be replaced.

Ultimately, it is a move toward PoS ["Proof-of-Stake"] that the developers see as a critical way to restore what was an original value proposition of decentralized blockchain networks, that anyone could participate simply by running a program on a computer.

Turing Completeness

As noted earlier in this book, ethereum is purportedly "Turing-complete", but in reality, the system is limited by memory, computation power, storage on the network and economic costs. The more complex the instruction set, the more messages that have to be passed back and forth within the system, the more delegates and code calls required by the contract, the higher the cost. The gas system ensures this. Ethereum, however, has an accompanying economic system of ether and gas that makes it, at least at the moment, prohibitively expensive to use. It creates an economic limit on the Turing-completeness simply by making storage space so expensive.

In some ways, ethereum can never really be a true Turing machine – at some point, a limit to computational power is hit, even if it grows to where the limiting factor or bottleneck is available electricity. But for ethereum to achieve its purpose, it only needs to reach a point of economic equilibrium where it is "practically" Turing complete and limited by the economics of how much it costs to use.

PROFERRED SOLUTIONS

Blockchain technology has ushered in a new age in distributed computing. There is a powerful belief that distributing formerly centralized systems will be massively beneficial, both in removing the potential abuse and making them more fault-tolerant.

But, distributed systems are inherently less efficient than centralized systems. They are generally also slower, more costly and more complicated. This must be the case, as when data is centrally stored, controlled systems do not need consensus layers. There is no computational power that needs to be spent to align the state of a centralized database across a broad system. This challenge is one that faces all public blockchains, and ethereum offers no specific or special solution to this dilemma, at least today. Yet, there are ideas being developed to attack this issue. From sharding and state channels to changes in the consensus algorithm, serious efforts are underway to find solutions that could allow ethereum to massively scale.

Technical Transition

One of the proposed improvements to ethereum's current design involves a unique technical feat that would find the network turning off its Proof-of-Work (PoW) transaction verification mechanism and replacing it with one based on Proof-of-Stake (PoS). PoW is a powerful consensus algorithm because it allows the system to prove that work was actually done to mine a block. PoS validation, on the other hand, doesn't use a mining process. Holders of the network's tokens own stakes in the network based on a percentage of ownership and vote to validate and include blocks in the blockchain. But, there are problems with PoS systems today. Should powerful forces gain the majority of ethers on the network, PoS could ensure these actors continue to have an outsized influence on the network. This would create a new upper class reminiscent of the landed gentry, a term that refers to a British social class able to support its lavish lifestyle purely from rental income. But there are benefits as well. If joining the network can be simplified, requiring only that the user download a program and hold a balance of ether, barriers to entry in the form of costly equipment can be all but eliminated. One of the architects working on this migration is Vlad Zamfir, and he is candid about the technical challenges of the current Ethash protocol, which he said: "doesn't scale". Put more simply, he said: "Everything about ethereum is going to have to change."

The Casper

Zamfir has so far spent 11 months researching, studying and testing out concepts to enable the eventual transition to PoS consensus. In August 2015, he made public a proposal for a new consensus algorithm that would be known as 'Casper', the name a nod to the fact that it is an adaptation of its existing GHOST mechanism, which replaces miners with 'validators'. These nodes estimate (based on what they can observe of the network) how the network state should look were they to verify all contracts, transactions, and changes in the ledger that have occurred since the last point of consensus. They then broadcast that guess to each other and evaluate what other nodes are broadcasting to them. As nodes recognize each other's guesses or votes, they begin to coalesce around a single network state. When the nodes are in agreement to some mathematical level, the network reaches consensus, and then records are updated in all nodes, including those that are not validators, and those validators who have not yet reached the same conclusion. One dilemma that has emerged has been termed the "nothing at stake" problem, whereby PoS validators have nothing to lose by voting for more than one blockchain history, which in turn precludes consensus. Since there is no mining, and little resource is used to validate transactions, it becomes comparably easier to try and solve several versions of the blockchain at the same time. Casper's solution to this involves bonding. Validators must post value in the form of ETH into a smart contract that monitors their validation process. By putting a value on the line, the incentive to "cheat" and validate multiple chains is eliminated by making it more costly to lose the bonded value pledged than it would be to gain a reward through cheating. Casper is being built to monitor the nodes and detect "dishonest" actions. When Casper recognizes a "cheater", it executes the contract to permanently confiscate the posted bond and bans the node from becoming a validator in the future. There will be several key benefits to this system, they include:

• A focus on CPU power rather than GPU power, making the network more egalitarian

• Better support for lightweight clients

• The capacity for more transactions per second

• The possibility of even faster block times.

State Channels

One partial solution, which doesn't actually scale the core protocol but does effectively arrive at an improvement, involves state channels. Put simply, state channels are a method of conducting transactions that could occur off of the main blockchain. This is a critical component that would be needed to scale the ethereum protocol. If state changes can be moved off of the ethereum blockchain, significant scaling becomes possible. It does, however, have to be done carefully to ensure that it doesn't add risk to the network's participants. This requires some system that would lock the blockchain state by a form of contract. In other words, in order to protect the participants in the off-chain transaction, both parties must be able to sign off on the validity of the transaction itself. The participants then must submit back the state created in the channel to the main blockchain, and the main blockchain must accept it as an update that necessarily amends and overrides the previously reported state from the channel. This would unlock the value that is being kept off-blockchain and allow it to move back on the blockchain, with the computational requirement for the state change having taken place off-chain and without creating a systemic burden. State channels could become a powerful solution to scaling and have benefits in other areas as well. For example, it could be seen as a way to provide heightened privacy. In the case of disputes, parties can end contracts without revealing what might have taken place.

Sharding

Still, there is another solution being developed known as "sharding" that has, at the time of the report, yet to be introduced in a public blockchain. In a sense, sharding attempts to leverage the insights of traditional database sharding, wherein portions of the full database are held on separate servers as a way to spread out the load and improve performance. When applied to a public blockchain environment, implementing this architecture becomes more difficult, albeit comparably beneficial.

The successful sharding of the ethereum database would allow for multiple blockchains to exist within the same network so that businesses, individuals or entities could run the equivalent of a public or private blockchain (with distinct transaction validators), but on a platform, that leverages the security and functionality of a public platform. By sharding the network into smaller chunks, the network state can be split, too. Each account will be its own shard, which will only be able to send or call transactions within the limitations of this environment. At the top level of the protocol, there won't be any major change, but underneath there could be a world of difference. Instead of the top layer of the network having to process each transaction and each contract, the smaller shards can be processed and then sent back to the top layer of the protocol. There, the state of the entire ledger would be updated with the processed information. Until this takes place, ethereum truly cannot be a practical platform because it is extremely inefficient. But, by distributing the computational load among the shards, ethereum may yet become suitable for enterprise-level applications.

Development Timeline

Ethereum has differed from other open-source blockchain projects in that it presented a detailed overview of its long-term roadmap early on in its development cycle.

First unveiled in March 2015, ethereum's timeline included four release steps, each with its own outline for what development changes would be needed to implement that vision. In the following section, we review those steps:

Frontier

Described as the ethereum network in its "barestform", it was 19 months after the project's initial debut that the genesis block in Frontier was generated on 30th July 2015. Frontier was the first version of ethereum, one described by the organization as a beta release aimed at developers who wanted to experiment with the project's tools. It offered basic command-line capabilities and provided users the ability to mine ether and upload and execute contracts. This was the tool to stand up key components of the ecosystem such as exchanges and app development projects.

Homestead

Presently, the most recent milestone cleared by the ethereum team, Homestead was described as the first "production version" of the network. Released on 14th

March 2016, Homestead still features a command-line interface but was framed as the first commercial iteration of the technology. Homestead was automatically introduced at block number 1,150,000 on the ethereum blockchain. Perhaps most notable about the launch was that it required the ethereum community to undergo the hard fork, a process by which a change was made to the network's consensus algorithm that invalidated a past rule, rendering nodes incompatible unless they upgraded. The feat further came at a time of deep contention within the bitcoin community about its ability to make such a shift and was widely seen as a validation of ethereum's development team and its decision-making abilities.

Metropolis

Anytime from now, the next major release of ethereum will be Metropolis. Though no set date for the transition has been announced, ethereum has always been a developer led the effort, and developer-led efforts don't necessarily stick to timelines. Metropolis will be the fully-featured version of the product, aimed at non-technical users, and will be the first official non-beta version. It will also include the first fully functional version of the Mist browser, providing a graphical user interface atop the client. This version is expected to bring fundamental back-end improvements and upgrades to Solidity. In many ways, Metropolis will represent ethereum version 1.0.

Serenity

It won't be until Serenity that we reach what the community is calling 'ethereum 2.0', a version of the platform that's ready to scale. Serenity will see major and fundamental changes in the way that ethereum functions as a platform and protocol. The first of these changes will be a migration away from the consensus algorithm currently underlying the ethereum blockchain. Ethereum will fork from a Bitcoin-like PoW mining process to one whereby holders of ethers validate the state of the network through a voting mechanism. In addition to the switch to PoS consensus, Serenity also plans to introduce scaling solutions including 'sharding' and 'state channels' to the ethereum protocol.

Latest News On Ethereum
Russian Bank Consortium Uses Ethereum-Based Ledger as Government Signals Support (03-08-2017)

A consortium of Russian banks is using an Ethereum-based blockchain to make payments faster and safer, according to Bloomberg. The banks, including VTB Group and Sberbank PJSC, have formed a distributed ledger called Masterchain that uses a modified Ethereum protocol. The ledger complies with the country's security standards, according to the FinTech Association, which the central bank backs.

Two months ago, President Vladimir Putin met with Ethereum's founder, Vitalik Buterin, signaling a shift in the government's position on cryptocurrency. Last year, the Finance Ministry threatened to arrest and imprison anyone using digital currencies. Vyacheslav Putilovsky, an analyst at Expert RA, a Moscow rating company, said Russia is a highly developed banking market, and the leading banks want to match if not overtake their western competitors in adopting such technology. Blockchain technology can be used to verify intellectual property rights, contractual agreements and public ledgers without intermediaries. The R3 consortium of U.S. banks in May raised $107 million from its members, which include HSBC Holdings PLC and Bank of America Corp. A distributed ledger could reduce costs for record keeping mortgage certificates by up to 80%, in addition to speeding business by removing intermediaries like public notaries, the consortium noted in a white paper. The Russian banks wish to begin applying the system for mortgages by mid-2018. The consortium also includes TSC Group Holding PLC, Bank Otkritie FC, and Alfa Bank.

A New Virtual Currency

A virtual currency known as "gas" will reward third party miners for validating transactions within Masterchain, according to the white paper. "Gas" is an abstract unit measurement for the resources needed to process one transaction and record it to the distributed ledger. It is also the nickname for Ether. Masterchain will require computing capacity in order to validate transactions. Masterchain could also allow the banks to search one another's database for blacklisted clients in an effort to reduce expenses and fraud risks. Russia's central bank has already implemented an Ethereum-based blockchain for processing online payments and verifying customer data with lenders. Putilovsky said the mood in Russia could reverse again. He said the central bank's position on cryptocurrencies remains muddled. He said the bank could play a key role either in developing the industry or in undermining it.

Virtual Reality Platform Decentraland Announces Crowdsale (01-08-2017)

Decentraland, an Ethereum blockchain powered virtual reality platform that allows users to create, experience and monetize content and applications, has announced a crowdsale. Taking place Aug. 8-16 for its ERC-20 token, MANA, users will be able to buy and sell virtual real estate, called LAND, and participate in Decentraland's virtual reality economy.

The token sale has a $20 million cap and will be followed by a continuous issuance stage. Ariel Meilich, Decentaland's project lead, said: "As the virtual reality market continues its rapid growth, we are excited to launch Decentraland, a new virtual economy, where content creators are incentivized and fairly rewarded for their contributions". He added that Decentraland enables low cost, direct payments among content creators and users with its native token, MANA.

Prototypes Available

Decentraland has prototypes available for public testing. It offers unlimited possibilities for virtual content creators, including games, art, education and health care applications. Developers can create and monetize applications on the platform. They can use MANA to buy LAND and other goods and services on the platform. LAND's value is based on its proximity to high-traffic hubs, as well as its ability to host in-demand applications. A property owner can host other users on their LAND and determine how they interact with the virtual world around them. While gaming, art, and social applications are anticipated within Decentraland, the protocol enables users to come up with other novel use cases.

Secondary Market Trades

Decentraland has teamed with district0x, a collective of decentralized communities, to provide users the ability to trade LAND in the secondary market. While unclaimed LAND can be bought at the same exchange rate (1,000 MANA = 1 LAND), differences in traffic and positions could allow LAND parcels to trade at different prices on a secondary market. Ownership of LAND is recorded on the Ethereum blockchain, assuring immutability, Meilich said. Interactions are recorded on a network of nodes streams, providing users full control of their LAND and their content. Decentraland has established financial incentives to support the utility value of the network. Contests for creating applications, art, games, and experiences will encourage content creators to compete for MANA. New users will also be provided allowances in MANA, allowing them to participate in the economy.

Meilich said:

"For example, communities hosted on offline and online forums like chat groups and centralized multiplayer games can transition to Decentraland and integrate economic capabilities into their communities." Supporters can participate in the MANA crowdsale with major cryptocurrencies via the ShapeShift exchange.

Crowdsale to Support Development

Funds raised in the token sale will be distributed as follows: 50% for development, 20% for research, 15% for community development and marketing, 10% for business development and operations, and 5% for legal costs. A continuous issuance stage will follow the crowdsale, allowing a decreasing percentage of the initial supply of MANA to be purchased from the smart contract each year, in limited supply over time. Decentraland will protect the token from inflation by requiring users to burn MANA to claim LAND. The board of advisors includes Luis Cuende, Aragon project lead, Jake Brukhman, CoinFund managing partner, and Diego Doval, creator of n3xt. Meilich concluded:

"The gaming market has demonstrated a strong demand for a decentralized community virtual world. Decentraland is confident that with our illustrious team of gaming, smart contract security and blockchain engineering experts, we will produce the first fully decentralized virtual economy that revolutionizes the gaming industry."

Ethereum Miners Lease Boeing 747s to Ship AMD Processors; Share Price Goes Up (27-07-2017)

Ethereum miners purchasing advanced micro devices (AMDs) are helping to push their share prices up with some miners leasing Boeing 747s to ship the devices out quickly for them to be plugged into the network. According to a report from Quartz, AMD shares rose by 11 percent on 25 July; however, over the last 12 months, the firm's stock is reported to be up by more than 152 percent. This makes it the fourth best performer on the S&P 500. Lisa Su, AMD's chief executive, said the company had seen an increase in the purchase of AMDs from digital currency miners. While management wasn't specific on how much, the [graphics processor unit] revenue upside was driven by cryptocurrency applications.

Leasing Boeing 747s

Ethereum, the second largest digital currency with a market cap value of $18.3 billion, has experienced an influx of interest from traders, in particular with the mammoth number of ICOs currently circulating. However, its value has seen a near 4 percent drop since yesterday when it had a market value of over $19 billion. Despite this, though, many investors are keen to take advantage of ethereum's gold rush. So much so that ethereum miners are leasing Boeing 747s to ship AMD and Nvidia processors so that they can receive them quickly. Marco Streng, chief executive of Genesis Mining, a major ethereum miner, said:

"Time is critical, very critical. For example, we are renting entire airplanes, Boeing 747s, to ship on time. Anything else, like shipping by sea, loses so much opportunity".

At present, the price of ether is floating under $200 at $195, according to CoinMarketCap.

Potential Profits Increase 40-Fold

Through the use of graphics processing units (GPUs) acquired from the likes of AMD or Nvidia, miners can make money. However, in order to mine a supply of ether each day, the miners are required to pay for the labor and electricity to run them. However, as Quartz points out the costs involved have remained stable while ether prices have climbed from $8 at the beginning of the year to over $400 in June, meaning miners potential profits have risen 40-fold. Streng added:

"Everyone began to realize this and wanted to get GPUS to get mining. The mining return has gone up by 40 but the hardware is still the same cost. This creates an incredible economic incentive for people to start mining".

Interestingly, it was recently reported that small-scale ethereum miners were selling their AMD and Nvidia GPUs. According to a report from Motherboard, sellers are claiming that mining is no longer profitable.

Russian Airline S7 Now Uses the Ethereum Blockchain for Flight Tickets (25-07-2017)

A Russian airline has announced that it is to use the ethereum blockchain to sell flight tickets with backing from the country's largest private commercial bank. In a report from regional newspaper Kommersant, Russian airline PJSC Siberia Airlines, known as S7, and Alfa-Bank began the project of selling airline tickets on the blockchain on Monday. According to the bank, one of the key advantages of employing the technology was the process of faster payments. Last December, it was reported that S7 had executed the first of its kind service payment using the ethereum blockchain smart contracts through a letter of credit with Alfa-Bank. The announcement of this latest project between S7 and Alfa-Bank comes after Russia's largest airline, Aeroflot, revealed that it had published a proposal for the introduction of digital currencies and technologies related to it into its operations. In particular, the airline is considering the possibility of using cryptocurrencies for flight ticket payments. It will examine the demands for the currency as a form of payment in addition to the risks associated with the adoption of them on a larger scale. The completion of the projects is expected by 10th December 2017.

Russia's Position on Digital Currency

Meanwhile, while Russia appears to be looking at the blockchain with favor – in the past ethereum founder Vitalik Buterin is reported to have met Russian President Vladimir Putin – it is still considering its stance toward bitcoin. In June, it was reported that the head of the

Central Bank of Russia had stated that Bitcoin was not to be considered as a currency, but that there were plans for regulating it as a 'digital asset.' Elvira Nabiullina, the governor of the Central Bank of Russia, said that the authority was 'analyzing' the possibility of regulating the digital currency; however, before regulation could take place more research into the understanding of it would first need to be done. Yet, she added that there were doubts as to the benefits that Bitcoin could bring to the economy. She said:

"We don't consider that bitcoin can be considered as a virtual currency. It's more digital assets with the regulation of assets".

Conclusion

There is no gain saying, ethereum has come to stay. Initially, critics thought it won't endure the test of time, here we are today, ethereum and its blockchain are still waxing stronger and stronger. It has even been seen to be more useful beyond the imaginations of everybody. And that is not all, ethereum has a massive potential for expansion in the coming years. It is still in its development stage as there are currently about 35,000 developers and more than 500 start-ups working on the platform. Big companies like Microsoft and BP are using it. Like all other digital currencies, it is built on the blockchain technology and it will never become obsolete.

More Books By George Icahn

Check out my Author Central Page:
http://www.cryptocurrencystudio.com/george icahn

BITCOIN:

Bitcoin Investing, Bitcoin Trading, Bitcoin Mining - The Complete Guide To Understanding Bitcoin

George Icahn

© **Copyright 2017. All rights reserved.**

No part of this book may be reproduced or transmitted in any form or by any means, electronic or mechanical, including photocopying, recording, or by any information storage or retrieval system without prior written permission from the author or copyright holder except in the case of brief quotations embodied in reviews.

Although the author has exhaustively researched all sources to ensure the accuracy and completeness of the information contained in this book, we assume no responsibility for errors, inaccuracies, omissions, or any inconsistency herein. Any slights of people or organizations are unintentional. Reader should use their own judgment and/or consult a financial professional for specific applications to their individual needs.

Table Of Contents

Introduction **291**
Cryptocurrency Secrets + Newsletter
....**296**
CHAPTER 1 ....**298**
   Who is Satoshi Nakamoto? 298
   What is Cryptocurrency? 300
   How Bitcoin Rose to Fame 306
   Bitcoin Legitimacy and Decentralization 312
      Bitcoin Legitimacy 312
      Bitcoin's Decentralized Nature 315
   Summary 319
CHAPTER 2 .... **321**
   Bitcoin Creation and Mining 321
      Bitcoin Creation 321
      Bitcoin Mining 323
   Bitcoin Mining Hardware 325
   Bitcoin Mining Software 327
   Mining Pools 329
   Mining Difficulty 330
   Bitcoin Wallet 331
      Paper wallet 333
      Software wallet 335
      Mobile Wallet 338

Web Wallet 338
Transferring Bitcoins between Wallets 340
Buying and Selling Bitcoin (trading) 340
    Buying Bitcoin 340
    Selling Bitcoin 344
    Selling Bitcoin online 344
    Direct trades 345
    Exchange trades 346
    Peer-to-peer trading marketplaces 347
    Identity 347
    Selling Bitcoin offline 348
Risks of Investing in Bitcoin 348
Summary 351

CHAPTER 3 352

Bitcoin Trading Guide 352
    The Basics 352
    Tracking with Mobile Apps 353
    Things to Avoid 356
Online and Offline Bitcoin spending 359
    Online spending 359
    Donating Bitcoin online 360
    Spending Bitcoin offline 360
What to do if you have a business of your own 361
Uses of Bitcoin 369
Contemplating the prospects of Bitcoin 373
Summary 375

Conclusion...377
More Books By George Icahn...........379

Introduction

One of the human's greatest needs is the need for money; we think about it, talk about it, and make plans based on it. It is the reason we wake up in the wee hours to start our day and come back home when the kids are asleep. We started formal education, moved through grade schools to high schools, then to colleges and other forms of higher learning like the university. Doing all of these mostly because we want to secure a suitable career in life, a career that will earn us decent money. Most of the times, we are either busy making money, spending money, complaining about the jobs that give us money or grumble about how broke we are—but what exactly is money? To many of us, it is no more than numbers on the screen or pieces of paper in our pockets. The value of money has been the same for most of us since we were born. Even though inflations and other awkward market trends like the spasmodic rise and fall in prices of goods affect us all, we still stubbornly believe that this money we use is the only way we can pay for things. No wonder we do not question our current financial system. This money is what we base our entire life on, and you will find it interestingly terrifying that the value of such money (the pieces of paper in our pockets or the numbers on the screen), and how much of it is in circulation, is controlled by only a small group of individuals dressed in suits, seated around a table.

Before money became a means of exchange and a tool for execution of contracts, during the dark ages, people used clay tokens to record transactions. The value that was placed on things was based on how these things will help us survive. Precious stones like silver and gold, even grains, all served as a means of exchange because they held value (as in the case of precious stones) and helped in our survival (grains). Soon, clay tablets were used to record transactions, and these clay tablets can be preserved for a long time. This was how it worked (thanks to archeological discoveries): it stated things like 'the bearer of this tablet will receive a specific amount of grains or precious stones at a particular time because he gave something to Mr. A or Mr. B". We can relate to that because the contents of these clay tablets are quite similar to the bank statements that we now have.

Soon transactions changed to the barter system—it is a direct exchange of things of value between the individuals involved. Here's an example of what the system is like—I have a farm on which I grow wheat grains and after my harvest season, I take my wheat grains to another man who has a cattle farm. I proposed that I will give him some wheat in exchange for cattle meat (beef) or milk. But that also posed another challenge. What if the cattle owner already has wheat grains? Then I have to search all over for a farmer who rears cattle and at the same time needs some wheat grains because all of a sudden, my wheat grains (the only means of exchange I have) has been rendered useless. The barter system was not too efficient and it was not generally accepted as a means of transaction subsequently. It was then understood that people needed a more convenient way to purchase any item. This proposed means of purchase will not just be convenient but will also be universal. It must hold value, it must be scarce, it must be rare and must be something everyone desires.

From the foregoing, currency can be anything that is rare, scarce, and desirable. And this also shows that currency does not necessarily have to be physical like the paper money we are used to today. Another thing is that the paper currency system is centralized, only a few number of people control the financial system, what the value of money will be and how much of it will be in circulation at a given time.

But is it possible to operate outside of this current paper currency system? Will you appreciate a place to safeguard your assets where governments and central banks have no control over it regardless of occasional awkward market trends and frauds or bailouts or inflations? Can we conveniently make investments without the worry that we could go bankrupt someday as a result of the fall of the financial control center? That is the aim of this book. It will give you a self-guided tour on Bitcoin and how it will provide answers to the questions raised. This book will provide you with an integral understanding of the digital currency known as Bitcoin, which is rapidly changing the way we view money and transactions made. It will give you all the information you need to get involved from the beginning to the end. To take it a step further, I would like to invite you to join my newsletter (found in the next page).

Cryptocurrency Secrets + Newsletter

Join my **FREE** Cryptocurrency Newsletter to start receiving more information related to everything FinTech. It will help keep you on track. You will also be notified about my new books (at a special discounted price).

The best part? When you subscribe, you will immediately receive my **"Cryptocurrency Secrets"** Report where you will discover exciting contents such as: *The type of cryptocurrencies available, strategies to invest, how to collect more bitcoin, and much more!* It's just my way of saying thank you for your readership!

Follow The Link Below To Subscribe And Get Free Instant Access:

cryptocurrencystudio.com/offer

CHAPTER 1

Who is Satoshi Nakamoto?

For those with a strong interest in cryptocurrency or cryptography, the name Satoshi Nakamoto is not strange. It is the anonymous name used by the person or group of people that founded, created and designed Bitcoin. He or she or even they were the original creator of the bitcoin's reference implementation. Nakamoto is also credited with the implementation of Blockchain's database. Nakamoto started work on the Bitcoin project sometime in 2007 and was actively involved in the project till December of 2010 when his Bitcoin project was tampered with. But the Bitcoin software was created properly in 2009. The truth is that the real identity and nationality of Satoshi Nakamoto has not been proved right to this day. Nakamoto has claimed that he is Japanese, currently living in Japan and born on April 5, 1975, but many believe that the real identity of Nakamoto is not of Asian origin but could be from a couple of cryptography and computer science experts, maybe of American or European descent. There are some factors that point to the fact that it was an intentional attempt by Nakamoto to conceal and protect not only his identity but also his network. No one can identify him outside of Bitcoin. Just months before the launch of the first block (Bitcoin operation), he created a PGP (pretty good privacy) security key that was encrypted and has never been used till date. He has ever published a non-bitcoin post from his cryptography mailing list even though he is a guru in the field. He has browsed and sent emails using TOR browser using an email address from an anonymous email hosting service and from a free webmail account. Some have also speculated that he chose the name 'Satoshi Nakamoto' specifically because 'Satoshi' can mean 'wisdom' or 'reason' and 'Nakamoto' can mean 'Central source'.

> **Commented [u1]:** Ever or He has never published a Bitcoin post.

There may be at least two reasons why the creator of Bitcoin has kept their identity private. No one figured Bitcoin will be a big hit this fast. It has gained so much popularity and has become a worldwide phenomenon. If their identity was known, he or she will likely be a cynosure of lots of attention, both from the public, the media and some governments.

Another reason could be protection from criminals. The total payout of mined Bitcoin as at 2009 was 1,625,500 BTC which may be worth over $900 million today. Since mining was done only by him at the time, it must have been precautionary to limit his or her own exposure.

But looking at what Bitcoin offers, the promise of a cost-effective transaction as opposed to customers being charged frivolous fees for both online and offline deals, as well as its decentralized nature, it doesn't really matter whether the true identity of its founder is verified or not. Even though no one knows exactly who he is, his identity is irrelevant and it is only useful for historical records.

What is Cryptocurrency?

According to a dictionary, cryptocurrency is a digital type of currency in which encryption techniques are utilized to regulate the generation of units of the currency and verify the transfer of funds, operating independently of a central bank; they are decentralized and provide a platform for personal wealth that is beyond restrictions and corruption.

Does that still sound vague? Let's try to break it down. First, it's important to understand that cryptocurrency is not something you can hold in your hand, which will inherently turn a lot of people off to it right away. So, let's get something out in the open right now.

Remember that those dollar bills (those pieces of paper) that you hold in your hands are not actually worth anything and in fact, they're not even real. The paper currency people can hold in their hands are just representations of worth, and the worth that is put on that floating flat currency is based on nothing more than the faith people have in it paired with how much of it is in circulation. Yes, paper money is printed, but it is still nothing more than digits and decimal points on a computer screen, as most of the money we use today is digitized. Furthermore, remember that the money you hold in your hands is not something you truly own—the bank owns it because each dollar you have has been loaned to the government with interest, and in effect loaned to you with interest. So, in that sense, the idea of owning some form of tangible paper money is absurd—it's just a faith-floating currency controlled by a private organization with its flat based own best interests at hand.

When we talk about cryptocurrency we're talking about a purely digitized currency. It is made using cryptography (the study and analysis of secret coding and coding methods), making it nearly impossible to counterfeit, and the way in which cryptocurrency came about is most interesting indeed, because it was and still is a rebellion against the current monetary system that many people see as corrupt, but necessary. Looking at how the American Revolution really came about—the colonies had their own money supply that was regulated by the public—it was decentralized and it was a currency of the people that was not subject to inflationary moves by a central bank. It was when they attempted to force the colonies into accepting The Bank of England that the final tipping point for the revolution occurred.

Cryptocurrency isn't much different in that sense. In the 1990's a movement known as "cypherpunk" emerged. Without going into much details, cypherpunk was a counterculture phenomenon made up of hyper-intelligent tech-savvy young people who were taking advantage of the early World Wide Web. With this counter-culture came a lot of new ideas, one of which was known as cryptocurrency based on the modern mathematical theory and computer science practices of cryptography.

Cryptography is the practice of creating algorithms designed around computational hardness assumptions. Basically, it is blocks (think of a mountain made of rock) with information inside (think of the information as gold inside the mountain) and the cryptographic security surrounding it is what keeps the information secure (think about a huge wall surrounding the mountain with armed guards on top with RPG's). It is a way to encrypt the information within the secured blocks, making it nearly impossible to break, even by the worthiest of hacker adversaries.

The idea the cypherpunk movement had was incredibly innovative, and not so different from the idea the Americans had when they set out to wage their revolution—what if we could create an alternative to traditional currency that required no central authority to administer it, that was easy to transfer, works across political boundaries, and belongs—once again—to the people on a public ledger? The idea was so powerful, that it started gaining momentum as far back as 1995 when Seth

Godin in his book "Presenting Digital Cash" wrote of Jon Matonis (a still popular contributor of alternative currencies for Forbes Magazine), "Matonis argues that what is about to happen in the world of money is nothing less than the birth of a new Knowledge Age industry: the development, issuance, and management of private currencies."

Andy Greenberg in his book, "This Machine Kills Secrets" also recounts the history of the 1990s cyberpunk movement, which paved the way for resources such as WikiLeaks and righteous hacker groups such as Anonymous who seek to expose corruption within government entities, financial institutions, and law enforcement. This early Internet crypto-anarchists saw a future world where cryptography secured personal anonymity and privacy would be available to the point where it threatened the authority of the state. As Greenberg explains, their key insight is that anything that can be done cryptographically without government oversight.

They imagined online markets for information where buyers and sellers transacted anonymously using untraceable digital cash—anything from state secrets to private credit reports could be purchased at the right price. From that time onwards, some small attempts have been made on behalf of individual developers to create this cryptocurrency. However, all those virtual currencies relied on third party intermediaries, such as bank or credit card companies to prevent "double spending". It wasn't until nearly 15 years later that somebody got it right and created the world's first usable cryptocurrency—Bitcoin—which relied on zero third party intermediaries and therefore became 100% decentralized, beyond the reach of a centralized body like the central banks. For an in-depth look into cryptocurrency check out "Cryptocurrency: The Complete Guide To Understanding Cryptocurrency". You can find it at: http:/cryptocurrencystudio.com/cryptocurrency

How Bitcoin Rose to Fame

Gradually Bitcoin is fast becoming more grounded as an acceptable currency or means of payment all over the world. People are losing faith in banks and the traditional paper currency it circulates. Notable investment companies and financial organizations are exploring this idea and have already began to buy up bitcoins. The media is talking about it more than ever and with each passing day; more governments are legalizing it and accepting it as a means of exchange and payments, even implementing it in other fields of financial operations. As more people are putting faith in Bitcoin, the value is increasing and it is making this digital currency more sought after in the business world today.

In June of 2011, Bitcoin market value rose to an amazing $32 USD. Looking at that value, it simply means that as at 2011, a single unit of Bitcoin could be exchanged for $32 USD. In 2012, this value fell by $2 USD to $30 USD and the value kept rising and falling over the course of the next 12 months. These observed fluctuations in the value of Bitcoin continued till sometime in February of 2013, when again the price of Bitcoin peaked at about $30 USD, and since then, the price kept rising till date. There was a period of sudden rise in the price of Bitcoin; as of April 2013, the price of a unit of Bitcoin was $266 USD. The period this book was being written, the price of a single unit of Bitcoin was $2,189.44 USD. That means if you bought a hundred units of Bitcoin in 2011 at $32 USD per unit at $3200 USD, by July of 2017 they will be worth over $200,000 USD. Last year, the market capitalization of Bitcoin was around $1 Billion USD.

Bitcoin is the first honest money we have had in a while. It is like a precious stone, it is nobody's liability. No entity stands behind it and it is not redeemable in an authoritative manner for anything. It is popular because it protects its owner from unnecessary taxation, theft, corruption and mismanagement, devaluation, and confiscation; the very things that make many people poor today.

Another factor to consider is the time Bitcoin was created. At the time, the US market was on the verge of an economic and financial collapse. The Lehman brothers had just gone down and investors were having some sort of economic nightmare. Then suddenly, an inventor, a software developer, the legendary but anonymous Satoshi Nakamoto published a paper called Bitcoin for a peer to peer payment method. The paper was titled: "Bitcoin: A Peer-to-Peer Electronic Cash System. The paper's abstract says that Bitcoin is "purely a peer-to-peer version of electronic cash" and it will "allow online payments to be sent directly from one party to another party without going through a financial institution. Digital signatures provide part of the solution but the main benefits are lost if a third party is still required to prevent double spending". He continued by saying "we propose a solution to double spending problem using a peer-to-peer network. The network timestamps transactions by hashing them into an ongoing chain of hash-based proof-of-work, forming a record that cannot be changed without redoing the proof-of-work. The longest chain not only serves as a proof of the sequence of the events witnessed but proves that it came from the largest pool of CPU power. As long as a majority of CPU powers is controlled by nodes that are not cooperating to attack the network, they will generate the longest chain and outpace attackers. The network itself requires minimal structure. Messages are broadcasted on a best effort basis, and nodes can leave and rejoin the network at will, accepting the longest proof-of-work chain as proof of what happened while they were gone".

The move came at just the right time and was a direct solution to the problems facing people who up until then had become frustrated with the financial system, its cumbersome processes and wanted a fast way out, or at least an alternative. No wonder when Bitcoin came to the limelight, everyone was shocked: majority with ecstasy while just a few with uncertainty. It was a step up from the then archaic, medieval process. It created a storm in the market, investors were happy and they repeatedly hailed it as the next big thing to happen following the internet. It took some time for people to come to terms with Bitcoin hitting the market and even now, all the experts that were skeptical at first and for a long time about the prospects of this digital currency are now already accepting it and are even playing major roles in publicizing it.

Why the sudden rise to fame in less than a decade of creation? It is the faith people have in it and the prospects it offers those who embrace it. Let us briefly look at the journey of Bitcoin so far and how it got here.

- **August 18, 2008:** bitcoin.org was registered as the domain name. Presently, this domain name is "WhoisGuardProtected", which simply means that the identity of the person who registered it is not public information.
- **October 31, 2008**: Someone with the name Satoshi Nakamoto announced on the Cryptography mailing list at metzdowd.com that: "I've been working on a new electronic cash system that is fully peer-to-peer, with no trusted third party. He then gave the link to the pdf file on Bitcoin, the now famous white paper published on bitcoin.org with the title Bitcoin- A Peer-to-peer Electronic System. This paper later became the bedrock of how Bitcoin now operates.
- **January 3, 2009**: The very first Bitcoin block, Block 0 was mined. It is referred to as the "genesis block" today and it contains the

text: "The Times 03/Jan/2009 Chancellor on brink of the second bailout for banks", maybe to act as proof that this Bitcoin block was created on that date or sometime after that date. It could also be evidence for relevant political commentary.

- **January 8, 2009**: The first version of Bitcoin software was announced on the cryptography mailing list.
- **January 9, 2009**: The second Bitcoin block, Block 1 was mined and it marked the start to the mining of cryptocurrency.

Another reason for the rapid rise to fame of this digital currency is the network's aggregate power. It has tripled over the last 12 months and this is because Bitcoin increases as its cost of production increases. The size of Bitcoin's mining network is determined by the price of each unit of Bitcoin. The larger the network, the more difficult it is to produce and the costlier it is. This presented a wonderful prospect for making money, hence the popularity of Bitcoin today.

Bitcoin Legitimacy and Decentralization

Bitcoin Legitimacy

Notable investors all over the world have been experimenting with Bitcoin and that has given people so much confidence and faith in it. As more respected individuals in the business world get involved with Bitcoin, more people are attracted to it, they view it as legal and authentic and that has boosted its legitimacy. Consider the early days of Bitcoin.

In May of 2010, a software programmer from the United States exchanged about 10,000 units of Bitcoin, that was only worth about a cent each for two pizzas. That turned out to be the first transaction done with Bitcoin. But 3 years later, he would have become an instant millionaire had he held on to those units of Bitcoin because by then, 10,000 units of Bitcoin was now worth a staggering $1.9 million USD. Also in March 2013, a US citizen purchased a used Porsche Cayman using just 300 units of Bitcoin. These were transactions done by ordinary citizens, but more was to come. There came some big names that invested in Bitcoin. Considerations of the examples will strengthen your confidence in Bitcoin with regards to its legitimacy as an acceptable currency.

Charlie Shrem was one of the first Bitcoin millionaires. When he was just 23 years old, he was an entrepreneur in New York City. He opened an upscale lounge in NYC and that lounge accepted Bitcoin as a means of payment—the first ever. His plan was simple; he saw the prospects of Bitcoin so he created a startup called 'BitInstant'. This startup made it easy for people to transfer Bitcoin funds quickly and with ease. This rapidly increased the number of people that started using Bitcoin as a means of payments and soon, these ones were using Bitcoin more regularly. They could now make payments with Bitcoin the same way they would using their bank debit cards.

Today, everybody knows Wordpress (the famous blog and website giant), OkCupid (the best dating site on the planet) and Reddit (popular Gold dealer). They have started accepting Bitcoin as a form of payment. Even now, eBay (a popular online shopping mall in the US) and PayPal (the world's most preferred online payment method) have been putting into consideration the possibility of accepting Bitcoin as a means of purchase. What about offline?

We can buy almost anything today using Bitcoin, from the gigantic items to the minutest of things. We can now purchase cars using Bitcoin as many car dealers and companies now accept Bitcoin as a currency. We can purchase houses and other landed properties with it as most real estate agents are now in tune to Bitcoin. You can now even pay for your hotel bills and order your favorite dishes at a nearby restaurant with Bitcoin. 'A Class Limousine' is a black car service based in New York and they freely accept Bitcoin as a means of payment as well.

Cameron and Tyler Winklevoss, the popular Facebook-claiming twins, purchased 1 percent of all Bitcoin back in early 2013 and they are richer today. Also, Andreessen Horowitz, one of Silicon Valley's most famous Venture Capital Firms, announced its intention to invest in OpenCoin—its first Bitcoin company. There are other notable investors that are clamoring for investments in Bitcoin, like the Lightspeed, Garlock, Union Square Ventures, all connected to Silicon Valley.

As the number of companies that invest in Bitcoin startups rises, it is expected that more retail locations (either online or offline) will start accepting Bitcoin as a means of payment, and it will become easier to trade in Bitcoin. This will boost its legitimacy as a type of acceptable currency worldwide. This will then have a significant impact on people's decision to embrace this innovation that is already gaining grounds and spreading like wildfire.

Bitcoin's Decentralized Nature

As noted earlier, the public is already growing frustrated and losing faith in the traditional paper-money system and the way centralized banks are treating people and their hard-earned money. Bitcoin is the world's first decentralized digital currency; it is linked to no single person or country, it is under no control of any central bank and it cannot be minted on plastic, paper, or metal.

The presence of intermediaries is the choke-point where the governments can apply pressure in the current centralized financial systems. Take for instance how the problem of double spending is addressed. They entrust an intermediary to keep a ledger (physical) of balances and they deduct a transaction amount from the payer's account and add it to the payee. Long process, stalling because of the involved third party and unnecessary transaction fees, are all problems this type of solution involves.

But with Bitcoin's decentralized nature, the problem of double spending is solved without any need for an intermediary. There is forever only one payer and payee for any particular deal, which makes it literal digital cash. It does this by a publicly distributed ledger of transactions across a peer-to-peer network. Simply put, there is a digital ledger that records all transactions so that Bitcoin spent by someone cannot be spent by that same person again. There is no single central authority keeping all the funds as this digital ledger is distributed across all nodes. There is also transparency as opposed to the now common calling for oversight into the actions of Federal Reserve accounts. Bitcoin transaction records are public and available to everyone connected.

There is no third party regulating the ledger, no governments, no banks, no organization can claim to be in charge of Bitcoin regulation; meaning that if you transfer Bitcoin funds to someone or to your wallet (we will discuss this later in details), no one can touch it, nor be affected by whatever economic condition's affecting your banks. It is completely untraceable by any entity as it is literally off their radar. It belongs to you 100 percent and no other body or person. As a result of Bitcoin's decentralized nature, people all over the world that witnessed, and possibly were victims of the economic recession of 2008 by losing their money, have begun investing in Bitcoin.

There are also cases of government tampering with bank notes. Here are some examples.

- In 2017, the Federal Government of Nigeria **confiscated** hard currencies in Naira, Dollars, Pounds, and Euros, belonging to individuals all in the name of fighting corruption.
- In 2016, Syrian refugees had their wealth **confiscated** by border guards.
- In 2016, Venezuela had 720 percent inflation and Bolivar **lost** about 90 percent of its value.
- In 2013, the Government of Cyprus **seized** up to 40 percent of its citizen's money.

- In 2008, Argentina **nationalized** $30 Billion in private pensions.

True, governments are not the only way people lose money, hyperinflations and seizing of funds are serious threats, but wealth can also be stolen by companies or individuals. It is time to give people more control over their wealth, and Bitcoin provides just that. Here are some advantages of letting people have control over their wealth:

4. **It accelerates innovation** - If building a new service or product will make people rich; it is likely that more people will try to produce new things. With more people giving innovation a shot, competition will rise, and we all know competition always brings out the best in people. There will be quality products in the market because people are guaranteed that no one can tamper with their wealth.
5. **People work harder** - When people are sure that their income is always safe, they will work hard knowing that they can make a better life for themselves and their families. But when wealth can be taken from people any minute

and without permission, it dampens both their hardworking spirit and their incentive to work harder.

6. **It attracts the best and the brightest** - When a particular field has proved to be a guaranteed path to success, people will try and invest in that field. If people in a specific geographical location are known to have control over their wealth, it is a natural pulling force to the best investors and the brightest organizations.

So, Bitcoin can solve virtually all the problems experienced in the financial system today. It is resistant to confiscation, less susceptible to hyperinflation, guarantees transparency, eliminates the need for a third party, doesn't waste valuable time and it grants all users a universal access. With Bitcoin, one of the fundamental human rights is the right to control one's wealth.

Summary

This chapter has helped us appreciate the power of this digital currency, Bitcoin. Not only have we seen how it originated, but we have also examined how it will make the financial system better and more efficient. A discussion of the legitimacy, its acceptance as a means of payment by notable investors all over the world, and its ever-increasing acceptance by online and offline retailers are amazing. We also noted that Bitcoin's most useful feature is its decentralized nature, which will solve virtually all the problems faced by the financial systems today and how it will mean total freedom for all agencies. But this is just the beginning—let us examine other vital things about Bitcoin; how it is created, the different types of wallets for cryptocurrency. How to buy and sell it, the best way to conduct business transactions using it. The next chapter discusses these points.

CHAPTER 2

Bitcoin Creation and Mining

Bitcoin Creation

How do new bitcoins come into existence? Let us compare Bitcoin to a precious stone, say gold, and think about how gold is mined. This can be applied to Bitcoin mining (we will discuss that in details in the next article) because it can be likened to how gold is mined. Initially, there were few challenges mining gold, but as time went on and more gold was mined, the mining process became more tedious. It all started when gold was discovered in a particular environment. Then, individuals with little or no experience or even with little capital could just pack up gold after merely digging a few miles down. It was just at the surface. As the process continued, it took more and more work to dig it out because gold is a non-renewable natural resource that takes thousands of years to create. Before, an individual with just an axe could do the mining all by himself, but with more gold mined; a single person can no longer do the job all by himself. Presently, mining demands a crew with enhanced digging equipment. How does that relate to Bitcoin creation?

In cryptographic technology, the miner here is an individual with a single computer. When Bitcoin started, an individual could download a specific software that worked at creating Bitcoin. The software chipped away at cryptographic blocks of information by attempting to solve mathematical problems. Once a mathematical problem was solved, the person mining got rewarded with a bitcoin. But as time went on, these mathematical problems that must be solved to get bitcoins became more difficult. It got to a stage where an individual with a computer could no longer solve these mathematical problems alone. A team was required. A single computer software could no longer perform this task of mining Bitcoin. Computers with specialized software designed to run round the clock were required in solving very complex mathematical equations in exchange for more units of Bitcoin.

Bitcoin mining can cost thousands of dollars to set up and maintain. Currently, every 10 minutes, 30 new bitcoins are created, and every four years that figure is halved. The cryptocurrency will increase in value over time and no centralized authority can inflate the supply of Bitcoin or attempt to devalue it. The creation of Bitcoin will continue till the final Bitcoin is created in the year 2140. According to permutations, only 21 million bitcoins will ever be in operation. The process of mining Bitcoin, as well as a discussion of recommended mining hardware and software, is the next topic we will give attention to.

Bitcoin Mining

Basically, Mining in this context refers to the addition of new block records (transaction) to the public ledger of blocks. We remember that these blocks make up a chain of transactions or blocks in that digital ledger known as the blockchain. Once these transactions are recorded, the blockchain makes it public to other connected networks or nodes of the completed block. The node connected to the blockchain network makes use of this information in differentiating between legitimate and illegal Bitcoin transactions or from attempts to re-spend bitcoins that have already been spent. Since the Bitcoin uses the "proof-of-work" function, each transaction or block must contain this hash cash "proof-of-work" in other for it to be considered authentic and acceptable. When the blockchain receives a new block, each node connected to the blockchain tries to verify this blocks' "proof-of-work", then on completion of this verification, validates the block or transaction. It only takes about few seconds to complete all these processes. Upon validation, the new block is added. In this way, the number of blocks added each day is kept in check and remains steady. It is resource-intensive and was specifically designed for this purpose. It allows each blockchain connected node to keep transactions secure and reaching a tamper-resistant agreement.

But mining is also used to introduce new digital currency into the system. When new bitcoins are created, miners are rewarded with the transaction fees. These new bitcoins are distributed in a decentralized manner and it builds confidence in the security of the entire system. Miners of Bitcoin assist in keeping the network secure by a consensus approval of transactions. Mining ensures fairness while keeping the network safe, secure, and stable.

One may ask though, how does the mining process work? Let us briefly take a look at the way hard currency or paper money is circulated as an example.

The government decides and gives approval on when to print the cash and how to distribute it. But the Bitcoin in this respect does not need a central government to approve its creation and circulation. We recall that it is a digital, decentralized currency and as such does not need a central government calling the shots. Miners use specialized software programs and specially designed mining hardware to create or mine these currencies. They use the software programs to solve arithmetic problems and in exchange for this, are issued a set number of digital currencies. It is a smart way to get the currencies and encouraging to others that are interested in mining these digital currencies.

Bitcoin Mining Hardware

The hardware for mining Bitcoin is designed to generate the "proof-of-work". There is much hardware to choose from, but your choice of hardware will be determined by a number of factors including the type of coin you want, hashing algorithm and the general acceptability of the hardware, in terms of user ratings. What exactly is the above-mentioned hashing algorithm or hashrate? It is the rate that controls how many attempts a miner makes in solving a Bitcoin block per second. The more attempts at solving a Bitcoin block, the greater the chances of solving the block and the better the mining hardware. The hashrate is measured in hash per second (H/s). We can have Kilohash (KH/s), Megahash (MH/s), Gigahash (GH/s), Tetrahash (TH/s), and the Petahash (PH/s). Below is a table that discussed the top three cryptocurrency hardware in details.

Harware name	Avalon 6	AntMiner S7	AntMiner S9
Hashrate	3.5 TH/s	4.73 TH/s	11.8 TH/s
Power usage	1050 watts	1350 watts	1350 watts
Power efficiency	0.29 Joules per GH	0.28 Joules per GH	0.1 Joules per GH
Controller	Separate	Built-in	Built-in
Noise	55 db	62 db	50 db
Chip process	28 nm	28 nm	16 nm
Breakeven point	7 years	2.6 Years	0.9 Years

Of course, there are much hardware to choose from. If you think of mining, the above ones are most recommended.

Bitcoin Mining Software

The major work of creating a digital currency is done by the mining hardware, but the mining software also plays an indispensable role. It is needed to link the Bitcoin mining hardware to the blockchain network. Similar to the hardware, a number of factors must be considered in choosing which software program will be useful for you in your Bitcoin mining process. These factors include the operating system and the type of cryptocurrency you plan to create. One thing to take note of is that there are upwards of 900 different types of digital currencies as of 2017 and each of these digital currencies has a specialized software for their creation. That means if you are planning on creating Bitcoin, for example, the software used in the creation of Dogecoin may not work for you. Although it must be noted that, some softwares can be used to create more than one type of cryptocurrency. Bitcoin mining software is straightforward—its the software you need to install on your rig that works to solve the cryptographic hashes. There are many Bitcoin mining apps out there including the following:

- ZOTAC 750 T 1GB (5.35 MH/s for Lyra 2v2)
- 50Miner – A GUI frontend for Windows (Poclbm, Phoenix, DiabloMiner)
- BFGMiner – Modular FPGA/GPU miner in C
- BTCMiner – Bitcoin Miner for ZTEX FPGA Boards
- Bit Moose – Run Miners as a Windows Service.
- Poclbm – Python/OpenCL GPU miner (GUI (Windows & client version of Poclbm (GUI)
- DiabloMiner – Java/OpenCL GPU miner (MAC OS X GUI)
- RPC Miner – remote RPC miner (MAC OS X GUI)
- Phoenix miner – miner
- Cpu Miner – miner
- Ufasoft miner – miner
- Pyminer – Python miner, reference implementation MacOS X))
- Remote miner – mining pool software
- Open source FPGA Bitcoin Miner- a miner that makes use of an FPGA Board

- Flash Player Bitcoin Miner – A proof of concept Adobe Flash Player miner
- XFX 7990 (21.8 MH/s for x11)
- XFX 7990 (28 MH/S for Quark)
- XFX R9 290x black edition (32 MH/s for Ethash)

Mining Pools

The last lesson in Bitcoin mining is that you should always join a pool of other miners, unless you have a ridiculously powerful mining operation and if that's the case you wouldn't be reading this book. Mining pools provide consistency and ease of Bitcoin acquisition. Essentially, it's a bunch of miners combining their resources, and sharing the spoils. Mining pools offer shares—a hash is easier to create a pool than solo, and it still provides proof that you have done valid work toward finding the next block. The more shares you can calculate and submit, the more fractional ownership you achieve in the next block reward (Bitcoin reward). Mining pools provide websites with stats and account management, which makes it easy to connect and monitor your hashing power and BTC generation. There are many mining pools out there available for you to join, and unfortunately, we can't tout any over another within this book. However, a simple Google search for Bitcoin mining pools will get you started.

Mining Difficulty

Simply stated, this is a measure of difficulty in finding a new block or how difficult it is to find a hash below a given target. The measure is periodically adjusted based on the hashing power that has been deployed by connected miners. There is a global block difficulty, so blocks that are considered valid must hash below this target. The difficulty is adjusted every 2016 blocks, based on the time taken to find the previous 2016 blocks. If one block is discovered every 10 minutes, it will take 2 weeks to find 2016 blocks. If the previous 2016 blocks took longer than 2 weeks to find, the difficulty is reduced. Conversely, if it took less than 2 weeks to find 2016 blocks, as expected the difficulty is increased.

Bitcoin Wallet

When we have money, we keep it in our wallets or purse. That is the same thing the Bitcoin wallet is all about. All bitcoins are stored in a wallet. A Bitcoin wallet is an electronic device that permits all forms of electronic transactions, be it purchasing items online or at a store. It can be used from a personal or shared computer or even from a smartphone. There is more, even your bank account can be linked to your digital wallet. It can also be used to store digital coupons or loyalty card information. Once your Bitcoin is revealed, you store them in a wallet. Just like we guard our normal wallets against theft or misplacements, so also, we take measures to protect our Bitcoin wallets because it can be stolen, or we can lose it if we are careless.

There are many ways to store our money. We all have bank accounts, and most of us have cash in our physical wallets. Both methods are used to store money meant for different purposes. The money in the wallet is for immediate use and the one kept in the bank account for long term use. Just like we have different storages for storing money intended for different purposes, we have different Bitcoin wallets to store Bitcoin meant for different purposes. Some of us operate multiple bank accounts, savings accounts, and current or checking accounts. Some have safety deposit boxes, while others own online accounts like Paypal or Payoneer. All these various ways of storing currencies have their advantages and disadvantages as well. Nothing is 100 percent secure in today's world. Our physical wallets can be stolen or misplaced, safety deposit boxes can be gutted in fire and banks can feel the impact of economic recession. So, a careful study of the various types of Bitcoin wallets is necessary so you do not lose your bitcoins. By learning the art of storing your bitcoins across different channels, you are protecting your income— as all your eggs are not being kept in the same basket.

Currency can be sent from one wallet to another, and basically, there are 4 types of Bitcoin wallets. They are:

- Paper Wallet
- Software Wallet
- Mobile Wallet
- Web Wallet

Paper wallet

This Bitcoin paper wallet is also called "cold storage" and it is the most secure of the four types of Bitcoin wallets because it lets you store your Bitcoin in any desired form of offline storage, independent of a computer, and that means hackers have no chance of reaching your funds, meaning they can't steal your money. Another advantage of the paper wallet is that computer viruses cannot tamper with your documents whenever you desire to store your Bitcoin, and you can keep it from everyone. Only you can access it as it is like your own bank vault. The only way of losing your Bitcoin is if you lose the safe, forget where you kept it or in cases of a natural disaster, maybe fire or flood. People generally make use of Bitcoin paper wallet as a long term saving vault for the cryptocurrency.

Earlier we mentioned that each type of wallet is different from others. Here is how paper wallet differs from other types of Bitcoin wallets. Every time you want to send or receive Bitcoin, or want to gain access to a Bitcoin wallet, you need a cryptocurrency address that is generated from a public key. Each public key has a private key that unlocks the address. The public key is like your bank account and the private key is like the Pin number that grants access to the bank account. So if someone were to have your private key, they can get to the bitcoins stored therein.

With any standard Bitcoin client, the private keys are stored in a file called "wallet.dat". This file is on your computer. If the file is not encrypted, anybody can have access to your private keys and a computer virus can damage the file. But if you encrypt it, you will need to supply a password every time you perform any form of transaction, or anytime you want access to the wallet. It is still vulnerable to keylogging. The idea behind a Bitcoin paper wallet is that if the internet never sees your private keys, then no one can trace it. To do this, the private keys are created online and printed out on a paper where it can be stored offline, someplace safe and where it can be accessed only by you.

Your private keys were never online and no one can hack into it. But you should take note that, if you misplace your paper wallet printout, or accidentally lose it somehow, then the currency stored on them will be gone forever unless you can recall them by heart in case you have a photographic memory. So what are your options? When you print out your private keys, store the paper wallet in a private deposit box or keep it in your bank. You could also put it somewhere in your home. You can also take a screenshot of the printout page and store it encrypted in an external hard drive. Even if someone sees it, they still need your password to view it.

Software wallet

This is the most popular way of storing bitcoins. This wallet is installed into your computer and you have total control of it. The security of this wallet is no one else's responsibility but yours. The disadvantage of this type of wallet is that if your computer crashes and somehow you lose all you stored on it, that automatically means your money is gone. On top of that, malware, spyware and other types of viruses that can attack your computer while it is connected to the internet can steal your bitcoins and so can any individual hack into your account. No wonder you have to take another security measure when deciding to use the software wallet. The following 2 security measures can help you protect your money.

3. **Encrypt your wallet** - This will make it safe from hackers and viruses. Anytime access to this wallet is required, a password needs to be imputed to decrypt this wallet before any transaction can be done. This will also protect the file on which your private key is stored, the "wallet.dat" file. Although it is still not 100 percent safe because some strong softwares like the keylogs can be used to crack your password codes. That is why experts recommend that you should own different types of Bitcoin wallets. They also discourage putting large sums of bitcoins in a single wallet. You can put a large sum in your paper wallet and keep a little in your software wallet.
4. **Back up your wallet** - This measure is good just in case your computer crashes. We all like backing up our files because we are not sure just when our computer will misbehave. If we can do that with files, how much more our Bitcoin wallets that holds our money. There are different ways of backing up our wallets. We can use external hard drives, while some have opted for online cloud backups. Just remember

that with any online backup comes the risk of hacking.

Let us now explore some software wallets that are recommended for easy use.

- **Bitcoin-Qt:** This is the original Bitcoin client and it is the backbone of the entire Bitcoin network, it has the highest security, privacy and stability of any software wallet. The only turn off is that it has fewer features and it takes up so much space on your computer.
- **Armory:** Armory is an advanced Bitcoin client and as the name implies, it is a software that offers protection. It has expanded features for power users. It offers backup features as well as encryption techniques, including cold storage on offline computers.
- **Multibit:** It is like bitcoin-Qt but lighter. Its focus is on being fast and ease of use. It synchronizes with Bitcoin network and in a matter of minutes, becomes active. It supports a variety of languages and is a perfect choice for people with little interest in technology.

- **Electrum:** This rare software wallet is all about speed and simplicity. It does not use up much of your computer resources or space and that is why many choose it. It uses remote servers that handle most of the complicated parts of the Bitcoin system.

Mobile Wallet

This is simply a mobile app that is linked or tied to a web wallet (we will discuss this next). They usually don't operate alone. It is like our bank's mobile apps that we use in checking our account balances. These apps will let you do the same thing you normally would do on a computer browser. They are available for IOS and Android users.

Web Wallet

A web wallet is the most convenient type of Bitcoin wallet out there and it comes with a greater security risk. Mt.Got, a popular web wallet has been hacked more than once, even though it has been responsible for 80 percent of all Bitcoin exchanges. As Bitcoin grows in value, so does the need for online security. As these fields are witnessing growth, it is difficult for web wallets to keep up with this growing demand.

Bitcoin power users only use web wallets for transfers involving only a small amount of Bitcoin, and for quick financial exchanges. They will rather opt for paper and software wallet to keep a bulk of their Bitcoin. For now, there are few web wallets that provide enough insurance to be used to store value like a bank. One advantage of the web wallet is that you can use Bitcoin anywhere with fewer efforts to protect your wallets. But there are good prospects regarding web wallets with its high potential of getting increasingly secure over time.

How you decide to store your digital currency is really up to how you intend to spend them. If you are thinking of investing long term, then it will be advisable to store a bulk of your Bitcoin in cold storage or paper wallet. If you are looking to make a simple and short-term investment, then the software wallet is your best option. If you are looking to make quick Bitcoin exchanges, then the web wallet and mobile wallet is what you need.

Transferring Bitcoins between Wallets

All the four types of Bitcoin wallets we have discussed so far (paper wallet, software wallet, web wallet and mobile wallet) have a Bitcoin address through which units of Bitcoin can be loaded. Just double check to confirm you are actually transferring to the correct address as you could lose your currency if it is done hurriedly, it is just like paying money into another person's bank account. Remember that with the digital ledger, a reversal is almost impossible in case you credit another person's address with your currency.

Buying and Selling Bitcoin (trading)

Having gone through how and where to store your Bitcoin, I believe it is time you try getting involved by contributing to this growing crypto-economy. In this section, we will give you a step by step guide to buying and selling Bitcoin.

Buying Bitcoin

It is no longer news that Bitcoin, the most popular cryptocurrency in the world, now has a growing number of applications and it is widely accepted by retailers around the world. So, it is very important to know where to purchase it as well as how to purchase it.

The first step to buying Bitcoin is finding a good wallet that appeals to you. Earlier we discussed what a Bitcoin wallet is—it is used to store your Bitcoin until the time you are ready to spend them or do any other transactions with them. We also saw the different types of Bitcoin wallets to choose from, and what should determine your decision. So, if you are planning to buy Bitcoin, try finding a wallet that fits what you want to use it for, and download it. It is recommended for beginners to choose a type of wallet that is easy to use and makes transfers a simple process. It is good news that these types of wallets are free to download, but when transactions are done, there may be currency exchange fees when transferring Bitcoin funds from one account to the other.

We have already discussed types of wallets, but in addition to the already discussed types of Bitcoin wallets, you should get to know about Mycelium, a popular mobile wallet (an app) that is known for its compatibility with more advanced techs, like the Tor and Trezor hardware. These mobile wallet applications give maximum security to your Bitcoin transactions.

After you have chosen the right type of wallet, the next thing you should do is choose the right Bitcoin exchange. Although most people decide to buy Bitcoin through a broker, the good news is that you can actually buy Bitcoin without a broker; all you need is an exchange. But you must be alert to identify fake and untrustworthy ones. Before choosing an exchange, find out more about their performance and what people have to say about them. Look at the fees they charge for each unit of Bitcoin that is bought and the supported payment methods. There are few exchanges that offer to turn Bitcoin units into cash directly, but not all exchanges offer this.

So how can you choose the right exchanges? The easiest way is to do a Bitcoin exchange search. You will be required to type in your country, and when you do, it shows lists of available exchanges you can choose from and also the latest "featured exchange". Don't rush through, take your time to analyze them all, check for reviews on each of them as well as their history (track record), before choosing anyone. Apart from doing a search for exchanges, you can choose from the exchanges that are commonly used by successful Bitcoin traders. Exchanges like the CEX, which gives room for simplicity and updates you about the current exchange rates and basic buy/sell options without any stress. It is to be noted that it offers limited payment options. Another exchange you can try is Coinbase, which is very easy to use and has amazing interface. it is available on mobile devices as well as on PC. This is always recommended for newbies.

The next stage is selecting a payment method. The different exchanges discussed accept a variety of payment options. They are choosy when it comes to payment methods because some payment methods have been used to defraud Bitcoin sellers. The generally accepted payment methods by most exchanges are credit card transfers and bank account transfers. Wire transfers are not accepted by some exchanges while PayPal is not accepted by some. There are designated ATMs that now allows you to exchange cash for Bitcoin but not all Bitcoin wallets are compatible. It is clear that direct dealings in cash are not acceptable payment methods by Bitcoin exchanges.

You are now ready to start buying Bitcoin and doing some real business with it.

Selling Bitcoin

One thing you need to understand is that selling Bitcoin is different from buying Bitcoin, so if you plan to follow the same steps you followed when buying Bitcoin, it won't work for you. When contemplating selling your Bitcoin, you must decide on how to sell it. You must select the most appropriate method for you—either sell your Bitcoin online or sell your Bitcoin in person. Each of the methods of selling Bitcoin has their own advantages and disadvantages.

Selling Bitcoin online

This is the general and recommended way of selling Bitcoin online. There are three ways of doing this namely:

- A direct trade with another person, with a third party making such connection possible.

- Selling through an online exchange, where your transaction is with the exchange rather than with the individual.
- Through a peer-to-peer trading marketplace that allows Bitcoin owners to get discounted goods and services with their cryptocurrency through others that want to purchase Bitcoin with their credit card. The marketplace provides a platform where both groups meet and solve their problems in a peer-to-peer exchange.

Direct trades

There are websites specifically designed for this kind of trades. When you open the website with the aim of selling your Bitcoin, you will be asked to register to verify your identity. After registration, you will be asked to post an offer, telling the website that you want to sell your Bitcoin. Anytime a buyer wants to trade with you, the website alerts you, and direct interaction continues between you and the buyer solely. You only use the website to complete your trade.

Exchange trades

This other way of selling Bitcoin online involves registering with an online exchange. Exchanges act as the third party or the intermediary who holds the funds. You only place the order to sell, the type of cryptocurrency you want to sell, and state the volume or amount of currency you wish to sell. You also inform the exchange the price per unit of the Bitcoin. When someone expresses their interest in buying the Bitcoin and later matches the 'sell order', the online exchange acting as the intermediary, proceeds to complete the transaction. They will then credit your account with the currency. But note that you must be patient in some cases as crediting the currency into your account may take some time, especially if your choice of online exchange is facing liquidity.

Some people alternatively use a pure cryptocurrency exchange to change Bitcoin for another type of cryptocurrency. While this is not too common, there are good reasons for trying this rare method, as there could be some shops that accept another type of cryptocurrency other than Bitcoin. An example is the Bitcoin shop that now accepts Dogecoin and litecoin as a means of payment for a wide range of goods.

Using some exchanges may require a small fee while there may be a limit to the amount of bitcoin you can store on an exchange. So, it is advisable not to store all your coins in an online exchange because they could be hacked.

Peer-to-peer trading marketplaces
These sites bring together two groups of people with specific but complementary needs. One group desires to use Bitcoin as a means of payment to buy stuff from websites which do not yet accept the digital currency. The other group wants to buy Bitcoin with a credit or debit card. This platform brings them together with their matching requirements so that they can now trade by providing Bitcoin to the one who needs to buy and providing discounted goods to the other. The marketplace acts as the intermediary by providing escrow for transactions.

Identity
It is important to discuss this briefly because some Bitcoin markets require a lot of proof to identify prospective Bitcoin sellers. There are legal requirements from the Bitcoin market to record who their users are, and thereby collecting data for future

regulations. So, when you first join the site, it is important to complete the identity verification process. This will make subsequent transactions a lot easier. You will be asked to upload scans of at least two utility bills that clearly display your name and address. The utility bills might contain your passport photograph or you may be asked to upload it separately. To sell your Bitcoin online, you must be ready to verify your identity.

Selling Bitcoin offline
This is by far the easiest way of selling Bitcoin. Simply scan a QR code on another person's phone and accept cash in return for the sold Bitcoin. So, in case, you have a friend who wants to buy Bitcoin, just help them set up a Bitcoin wallet, send them the cash, they get notified of the transfer of Bitcoin funds, and you get paid.

Risks of Investing in Bitcoin

Well, like every investment, Bitcoin carries certain risks. Although the list below are the risks of Bitcoin, they are not meant to discourage anyone from trying it out. They are just something to look out for.

1. High volatility

The price of Bitcoin has a high volatility. Typical 30-day volatility is around 40 percent and a 90-day volatility is close to 70 percent. These swings in value are hard to stomach for many people. Although the cryptocurrency has an uptrend, it's still risky.

Good currencies have low volatility, as owning unstable currency, or accepting it as a form of payment becomes too risky.

2. Government regulations

If the government decides to declare owning Bitcoin illegal, you may find yourself in trouble. Currently, the government stance on cryptocurrencies is not clear. And the danger is real as Bitcoin is not taxed, and is somewhat of a competition to the government issued currency. Other regulations could also make Bitcoin less attractive.

3. Competition

Other cryptocurrencies could send Bitcoin into history. Offering faster transactions, complete anonymity, storage space and other improvements could lead to lower market share for Bitcoin. If we consider the high quality of emerging cryptocurrencies, this scenario seems plausible.

4. Security of services/products

To use Bitcoin, you need wallets, exchanges, payment processors, etc. Not all of these services have perfect security. And if your funds are stolen, all you can do is to hope your service provider will be kind enough to give you refund.

Mt. Gox is the worst example, where thousands of users were left without their funds after a big hacking attack.

5. No safety mechanisms

Bitcoin has no safety mechanisms. Typically, you'll get a private key or random words which protect your wallet. If you lose your key, your funds will be gone with it. There's no support to contact, no way to change the password, and no way to verify your identity to get your account back. When it's gone, it's gone—there's nothing anyone can do.

Summary

The just concluded chapter's aim is to let you know how Bitcoin operates and to set you up for your first transaction in Bitcoin. I believe hearing about Bitcoin is not enough and learning about it only is not advantageous. That is why I took it upon myself to take you through the concept of wallets and how to buy and sell. We also learned how to create or mine ourselves. In our next chapter, we will talk about some additional tricks of making money, the users of Bitcoin in various fields and the future prospect.

CHAPTER 3

Bitcoin Trading Guide

The Basics

Bitcoin isn't as crazy and complicated like people think it is. It is not like the stock market with its big computer screen and complicated graphs and charts. Just anybody can trade in Bitcoin and be successful in it. Truth is said, it requires patience and good advice from those who are vast in Bitcoin trading knowledge. Another important thing to do about Bitcoin trading is to stay up-to-date as to current market news and the rise and fall of the price of Bitcoin as observed in the market.

Try to follow live Bitcoin market charts. Studying the chart will help you see the current price of a unit of the digital currency, the day's highest price and the day's lowest price, and the live market movements. The chart will help you know the cumulative volume of bid orders and the market depths—that is how much bitcoins would need to be sold for the price to either go up or drop down. The chart will also give you the cumulative ask orders and its market depth—that is how many bitcoins would need to be purchased for the price to move in a particular direction. But in all, the most important thing to look for in the chart is the current price of Bitcoin.

Tracking with Mobile Apps

The Bitcoin market is highly unstable with prices going up and down, it is important to keep track for you to be successful in trading. That means a close monitoring of the charts. We all have other things to do and it will be hard staying in front of the computer screen for 24 hours a day, 7 days a week. Some of us trade with Bitcoin part time or just in our free time while holding down a normal full-time job. To help us meet this need, there are great mobile apps that are designed to give us prompt notifications in case the market value of Bitcoin either goes up or down so that we can take a specific action. This way, we will know when to buy and when to sell (we know it is a good time to buy when the value goes down and to sell when the value goes up in order to make some profit).

Here are some mobile apps that can do that:

Go Bit Go – This is a free service that will text or email you when the Bitcoin price in your chosen currency hits a certain value, which you pre-select.

For example, if you want to be notified when Bitcoin goes up 20%, you can set that option. Alternatively, you can do the same if the price falls so that you are always prepared to act during important market changes. You can also be notified of what's going on with various exchanges including BTC-E, Mt.Gox, and Vircurex.

CoinCliff – This app takes a slightly different approach. It works similarly to an alarm clock. It will notify you of any pre-selected changes in Bitcoin prices. In addition to alarms, the app can also be set for regular notifications such as ones that are displayed when text messages are received. The CoinCliff app takes its data from Mt.Gox but is planning to add more exchanges such as BTC-E and Bitcoin-central.

Bitcoin Paranoid – In addition to this app displaying the current value of Bitcoin in USD, it also supports alarms.

Bitconium – This app supports alerts and takes real-time information from the following exchanges: MtGox, Cavirtex (Canadian Virtual Exchange), BTC-E, Bitstamp, and CampBX.

Of course, these aren't the only apps available. Depending on the kind of mobile device you have, android, blackberry or IOS, you can search your app store for similar apps that fit your need.

Do more than just invest, SPEND—Think about this in terms of a credit or debit card. You know that good credit is important because some day it will allow you to put a down payment on a house or a car or obtain a loan for a business. To have good credit, you can't simply get a credit card and not use it. On the contrary, you have to purchase things with that credit card and then pay it back on time and in full in order to build your credit rating over time. By doing this, you build faith among the credit agencies in that you are a responsible person who pays back any accumulated debt in a timely manner—this makes you a safe and worthwhile investment. Bitcoin is not too different. To make Bitcoin a safe and worthwhile investment in other people's minds, then it has to be used more regularly. This means that individual investors need to spend it as much as possible and not just trade it amongst themselves. Just like a credit card—you don't need to buy big things to give yourself a higher credit rating, you may just go out and buy your groceries on credit once a week. With Bitcoin, you need to make sure that you make a donation with it or buy something with it—exercise your Bitcoin spending rights. By doing so, you add more value to the currency and collectively help to stabilize its growth. If you're a business owner, make an effort to accept BTC as payment and encourage your customers to get into it. The larger the BTC economy becomes, the more sustainable it will be and the harder it will be to destabilize.

When it comes to Bitcoin, its continued popularity and whether it will increase in value really comes down to the actions of investors. For BTC to become more stabilized, more investors need to not only put faith in it, but more individuals need to spend it regularly and make an effort to do so. By doing this, Bitcoin continues to increase in value as it becomes more popular.

Things to Avoid
One thing to avoid is the idea that if everybody is following one particular trend, then we must go with the flow. This is in effect, making decisions and relying on the expectations of the people surrounding

us. For most of us that have tried it, we find out that the result is not what we expect. That is why we notice today that people buy some things, not because they need it but because they see everybody buying it; and eventually when they realize that they don't really need it, they start selling it off. In Bitcoin trading, it could have a lot of consequences, and could even result in the disappointments that accompany a considerable loss of funds. If you plan to trade with bitcoins, do not follow the crowd.

Another thing you should endeavor to avoid is freaking out when everybody is freaking out. Imagine a herd of cattle, relaxing in the middle of an open field. Just suddenly one of them raises a false alarm and starts running towards a particular direction. What do you notice about the others? The entire herd starts snorting and running toward the same direction. This trend too could be highly consequential in the marketplace. This happens when the market crashes or bubbles form. Just relax, take a break, because it may not be as bad as it seems.

Don't just believe all the information about Bitcoin that you come across. We are living in a period marked by information virtually everywhere we turn to, internet, TV, radio e.t.c. A wise Bitcoin investor will not put faith in everything said but will test out the credibility of news before acting on them. This is evident when an investor notices that generally, the price of Bitcoin goes down, and out from the blue comes news that there is a rise. He makes no research to find out whether it is true or not, he then makes a business decision based on the illusion that things are getting better. Of course, we expect the future of such investment to be shaky.

Avoid the ostrich effect. An ostrich can bury its head in the sand and believe it is invisible. That is a case of denial. Sometimes, new ones coming into the system focus only on their goal of making money that they do not or fail to accept the reality of current or future events relating to Bitcoin marketing.

And lastly, avoid overconfidence. An overconfident investor will always believe that their decisions are flawless. They refuse to ask questions where necessary out of pride and they are quick to condemn other people's business move. When they are confronted with their own failings, they either shift the blame away from themselves or they get angry. Instead of that all, learn to trust others and endeavor to learn from them. There is no Mr. Know-it-all.

Online and Offline Bitcoin spending

Online spending

The internet is the natural environment for Bitcoin spending because it is a digital currency. No wonder we trade bitcoins online in large quantities. Many online stores now accept Bitcoin as a means of payment. For the few ones that do not accept it, relax, there is always a way around it. There are websites that can be used to buy anything over the internet from any retailer whatsoever, even if they do not accept bitcoins. These websites do charge for their services as well, but the fees are really low. Examples of such websites are "bitspend.net", "opecoli.com", and "bitcoinrunner.com". Their transaction charges are as low as $3 or less per order no matter how much such orders are.

Anytime you want to make a purchase online, always make it a point of duty to check and confirm that they accept Bitcoin as a means of payment. You will be surprised to see how easy your online transactions will become. Trading in Bitcoin (buying and selling Bitcoin) is fun and simple, not only will it benefit you but also add to the stability of the digital currency.

Donating Bitcoin online
If you are passionate about philanthropy, then it will interest you to know that some charity organizations now accept Bitcoin donations. So, whenever you want to donate to charity, it will be wise to first check to see if they accept Bitcoin. Or you can ask them if you don't know how to check. Even politicians can look to use this mode of donation.

Spending Bitcoin offline
Earlier, we talked about the growing list of offline retailers who now accept Bitcoin as a means of payment. Just as in the case of online Bitcoin spending, try to ask your local retailers whether they accept Bitcoin as a means of payment. There will be some retailers that have not heard about this digital currency, and as such, do not accept it presently. You can help spread the word by explaining what Bitcoin is to them and how to use it.

What to do if you have a business of your own

What can you do if you have a business of your own? How can you contribute your own little quota to the legitimacy of this digital currency and help expand its borders? How can you help strengthen the economy of Bitcoin? There is no other way than accepting it for payment in your business. Take a look at PayPal, Payoneer or your normal credit/debit card, many businesses accept funds via these media today, but what if they all accepted Bitcoin for payments? By now the economy of the Bitcoin ought to have become stronger. So, if you accept it in your business, it will encourage more people to use and embrace Bitcoin trading and in effect spread the currency.

A point of caution is that you shouldn't hold on to Bitcoin payments in Bitcoin form for too long if you are a retailer, except you are planning to save it for long term purposes. This is because of the unstable nature of the digital currency. Earlier we talked about how the price fluctuates in the market. If you accept a Bitcoin payment today and hold it for too long in Bitcoin form, if the price drops it will result in a loss. So, my advice for you is that, as a retailer, when you accept Bitcoin as a payment, you should exchange the Bitcoin payment for cash. We talked about that earlier in the book. This can be done on your smartphones using mobile apps that were designed for this purpose through your chosen exchange.

But if you accept Bitcoin as a form of payment, are there any advantages? One major advantage is the elimination of the unnecessary and annoying charges that come with credit card transactions. Some of the fees are the authorization fees, sign-up fees, processing fees, ATM fees, annual maintenance fees, minimum balance fees, international currency fees, compliance fees, overdraft fees, paper statement fees and late fees. And you may wake tomorrow to find out that another kind of fee has been added. But using the Bitcoin as a payment method only has one fee, the processing fee and that's it. Also, Bitcoin payment is usually more secure than payments made with a credit card because it is like paying cash for an item versus information that can be stolen by a third party.

You can go about the process of setting your business up for receiving payment in Bitcoin by using the designed applications (third party applications) that will help you do this. The following examples are stores that allow Bitcoin payments.

WordPress.com—An online company that allows users to create free blogs
Overstock.com—A company that sells big ticket items at lower prices due to overstocking
Subway—Eat Fresh
Microsoft—Users can buy content with Bitcoin on Xbox and Windows Store
Reddit—You can buy premium features there with bitcoins
Virgin Galactic—Richard Branson's company that includes Virgin Mobile and Virgin Airline
OkCupid—Online dating site
Tigerdirect—Major electronic online retailer
Namecheap—Domain name registrar
CheapAir.com—Travel booking site for airline tickets, car rentals, and hotels
Expedia.com—Online travel booking agency
Gyft—Buy gift cards using Bitcoin
Newegg.com—Online electronics retailer now uses BitPay to accept Bitcoin as payment
1-800-FLOWERS.COM—the United States based online floral and gift retailer and distributor

Fiverr.com—Get almost anything done for $5
Dell—American privately owned multinational computer technology company
Wikipedia—The Free Encyclopedia with 4 570 000+ article Steam—Desktop gaming platform
The Internet Archive—web documentation company
Bitcoin.Travel—a travel site that provides accommodation, apartments, attractions, bars, and beauty salons around the world
Pembury Tavern—A pub in London, England
Old Fitzroy—A pub in Sydney, Australia

The Pink Cow—A diner in Tokyo, Japan
The Pirate Bay—BitTorrent directories
Zynga—Mobile gaming
Tesla—The car company
4Chan.org—For premium services
EZTV—Torrents TV shows provider
Mega.co.nz—The new venture started by the former owner of MegaUpload, Kim Dotcom
Lumfile—Free cloud base file server—pay for premium services
Etsy Vendors—93 of them
PizzaForCoins.com—Domino's Pizza signed up—pay for their pizza with bitcoins

Whole Foods—Organic food store (by purchasing gift card from Gyft)

Bitcoincoffee.com—Buy your favorite coffee online

Grass Hill Alpacas—A local farm in Haydenville, MA

Jeffersons Store—A street wear clothing store in Bergenfield, N.J

Helen's Pizza—Jersey City, N.J., you can get a slice of pizza for 0.00339 Bitcoin by pointing your phone at a sign next to the cash register

A Class Limousine—Pick you up and drop you off at Newark (N.J.) Airport

Seoclerks.com—Get SEO work done on your site cheap

Mint.com—Mint pulls all your financial accounts into one place. Set a budget, track your goals and do more

Fancy.com—Discover amazing stuff, collect the things you love, buy it all in one place (Source: Fancy)

Bloomberg.com—Online newspaper

Humblebundle.com—Indie game site

BigFishGames.com—Games for PC, Mac, and Smartphones (iPhone, Android, Windows)

Suntimes.com—Chicago based online newspaper

San Jose Earthquakes—San Jose California Professional Soccer Team (MLS)

Square—Payment processor that helps small businesses accept credit cards using iPhone, Android or iPad

Crowdtilt.com—The fastest and easiest way to pool funds with family and friends (Source: crowdtilt)

Lumfile—Server company that offers free cloud-based servers

Museum of the Coastal Bend—2200 East Red River Street, Victoria, Texas 77901, USA

Home Depot—Office supplies store

Kmart—Retail products store

Sears—Clothing, household products and electronic store

Gap, GameStop, and JC Penney—have to use eGifter.com

Etsy Vendors—Original art and Jewelry creations

Fight for the Future—Leading organization finding for Internet freedom

i-Pmart (ipmart.com.my)—A Malaysian online mobile phone and electronic parts retailer

curryupnow.com—A total of 12 restaurants on the list of restaurants accept bitcoins in San Francisco Bay Area

Dish Network—An American direct-broadcast satellite

service provider

The Libertarian Party—United States political party

Yacht-base.com—Croatian yacht charter company

Euro Pacific—A major precious metal dealer

CEX—The trade-in chain has a shop in Glasgow, Scotland that accepts Bitcoin

Straub Auto Repairs—477 Warburton Ave, Hastings-on-Hudson, NY 10706—(914) 478–1177

PSP Mollie—Dutch Payment Service

Intuit—an American software company that develops financial and tax preparation software and related services for small businesses, accountants and individuals.

ShopJoy—An Australian online retailer that sells novelty and unique gifts

Lv.net—Las Vegas high-speed internet services

ExpressVPN.com—High speed, ultra secure VPN network

Grooveshark—Online music streaming service based in the United States

Braintree—Well known payments processor

MIT Coop Store—Massachusetts Institute of Technology student bookstore

SimplePay—Nigeria's most popular web and mobile-based wallet service

SFU bookstore—Simon Fraser University in Vancouver, Canada

mspinc.com—Respiratory medical equipment supplies store

Shopify.com—An online store that allows anyone to sell their products

Famsa—Mexico's biggest retailer

Naughty America—Adult entertainment provider

Mexico's Universidad de las Américas Puebla—A major university in Mexico

LOT Polish Airlines—A worldwide airline based in Poland

MovieTickets.com—Online movie ticket exchange/retailer

Dream Lover—Online relationship service

Lionsgate Films—The production studio behind titles such as The Hunger Games and The Day After Tomorrow

Rakutan—A Japanese e-commerce giant

Badoo—Online dating network

RE/MAX London—UK-based franchise of the global real estate network

T-Mobile Poland—T-Mobile's Poland-based mobile

phone top-up company

Stripe—San Francisco-based payments company

WebJet—Online travel agency

Green Man Gaming—Popular digital game reseller

Save the Children—Global charity organization

NCR Silver—Point of sales systems

One Shot Hotels—Spanish hotel chain

Coupa Café—Coffee and Tea in Palo Alto

PureVPN—VPN provider

That's my face—create action figures

Foodler—North American restaurant delivery company

Amagi Metals—Precious metal furnisher

These examples show that there is a growing list of stores that accept this means of payment. So, what are you waiting for? Now is the time to come on board.

Uses of Bitcoin

With the Bitcoin phenomenon showing no sign of slowing down, it is about time you get with the program and get involved. An investment in Bitcoin offers you security and a guaranteed return on your investments as well as lots of easy and convenient ways to pay.

If you haven't already dabbled in this hi-tech world then we suggest you get with it and see what all of the fuss is about. Here are just 3 things the Bitcoin can be used for.

Day to Day purchase- While the above uses are special-interest uses, the average Bitcoin user will simply use Bitcoin to purchase basic goods from online (or even physical) retailers. As the Bitcoin market size grows, this will become increasingly common—the monetary value of Bitcoin will (theoretically) stabilize, consumers will want to spend their bitcoins, and retailers will see the benefits of accepting Bitcoin transactions.

This is a positive development for a few reasons. First, the low transaction costs mentioned above are a great incentive for businesses to accept Bitcoin payment; merchants can significantly cut their costs by reducing the fees involved in credit card transactions, authorizations, statements, interchanges, and customer service fees.

Second, the unique properties of Bitcoin as a currency makes it so the new payment system acts as a stimulus for financial innovation; features, such as micro-payments, which are generally not possible in other financial systems, create new financial opportunities and drive for new online business models and marketing strategies.

Cheap money transfer- One of the biggest pros of Bitcoin is that, compared to other electronic payment systems, it has a very low transaction cost. Bitcoin's transaction fee is not nearly as costly as the fees on money transfers brokered by banks, credit cards, and commercial softwares like PayPal.

The low costs of Bitcoin transactions are especially advantageous for immigrants sending remittance to their families in their home countries. This is a huge potential demographic for Bitcoin simply because the remittance transfer industry is quite large (about $542 billion was transferred globally in remittance flow in 2013). International transfers can be extremely expensive; in fact, according to the World Bank's report on Remission Prices, the global average fee for such payments was 7.72% during the first quarter of 2015. Also, such remittances can take significant amounts of time to be verified by the brokering financial institutions. Bitcoin allows immigrants to send cheap, practically-instant remissions. As of April 2015, the average fee per transaction was 0.000155 BTC (at the time, approximately $0.04 per transaction). The average time between transaction blocks was about 9.11 minutes.

Handling private expenses - One of the biggest pros of Bitcoin is its pseudonymous quality (members are identified by the public keys rather than their "real world" identities). For many people, this affords a desired level of privacy that traditional digital payment systems do not. Some examples of situations in which this quality really comes into play include situations in which people are fleeing from abusive partners, desiring controversial health procedures, or operating outside the confines of oppressive governments. Unfortunately, there is also the flip-side of this privacy; capability for Bitcoin to be used for unethical and criminal purposes. The most infamous example of this is Silk Road—the massive "Deep Web" marketplace. Silk Road used the privacy inherent in

Bitcoin (as well as an anonymous software called TOR) to allow users to buy and sell contraband. While the moderators of Silk Road didn't allow for the sale of goods resulting from or intended to cause the harm or exploitation of other people, users could still illegally purchase contraband such as illicit drugs and forged identity documents. Bitcoin's relative anonymity could also potentially provide criminals with avenues for money laundering or funding terrorist organizations.

Contemplating the prospects of Bitcoin

The future of Bitcoin is still clouded as the entire economic and financial community has mixed opinions about its viability as a currency. However, going by the current trends of growth in their use, the potential of Bitcoins as a currency seems to be rising. One should, however, ask this question "If the Federal Reserve creates more money in 2 hours than has been created by Bitcoin since its inception 4 years ago, what is riskier?" As Bitcoin is gaining popularity, more governments are taking a stance either for or against it. The Reserve Bank of India, for example, has issued a warning that use of bitcoins for money transfer is highly unsafe due to potential security and money laundering risks. The Government of China has taken a stricter stance by prohibiting payment and financial institutions from accepting them as payment. The European Banking Authority has also issued a warning that Bitcoin lacks consumer protection. Many more governments and central banks have also banned the use to prevent black marketing and alleged drug dealers that are using Bitcoin.

A lack of access to basic amenities like health care and insurance in developing countries is due to lack of income. The money required to have access to these amenities is more than what they make. Also, insurers tend to exploit these low-income earners by siphoning them and increasing the money unnecessarily. Bitcoin will ensure that these processes will be restricted to an online mode which will reduce the corrupt insurer's impacts. It will also give customers the option of paying in smaller amounts.

Other questions regarding the prospects of Bitcoin include: will Bitcoin or the technology that powers it ever be hacked? What if it crashes? Will the government shut it down one day?

We should remember that Bitcoin has already been reckoned with, and based on this it has already built a self-defense mechanism. Bitcoin network is made up of thousands upon thousands of computers throughout the globe, so a group of hackers will need mega synchronization to facilitate a take-over of this peer-to-peer network. In one word, it will never be hacked.

The fear that the government will one-day brand Bitcoin as illegal currency, and shut it down is unfounded. The truth is that, governments are already working with Bitcoin and will keep working with it. If the government has no trust in it, Bitcoin will not be trusted to help with the numerous operations of some governments today.

Summary

We have seen in the chapter how Bitcoin can be utilized and harnessed. Further impetus was given to using our own businesses to promote awareness of this easy and stress-free way of making payments. A discussion of the ways of setting up such initiative has been helpful, no doubt. By now, you will have been equipped to forge ahead and continue your online transactions with renewed vigor. Make good use of the information in this book, and take your business to the next level. You just may have identified your next business jackpot.

Conclusion

The rate at which Bitcoin is growing is amazing, and it is changing today's business world. No one can see the future, but one thing is sure—Bitcoin has come to stay. Bitcoin has paved the way for other types of useful cryptocurrencies as we now have over 900 different kinds of digital currencies. The advantages are numerous, more people are seeing the good it offers, and wise business experts have already seen the future as something bright. Although there are some who still don't know much about it, it is your responsibility to let them know. One way is by making it a means of payment in your organization. Bitcoin is gradually changing the way our economy works in a way similar to how the internet changed the way people access information. Remember, no government can ever shut it down, and its legitimacy will keep getting stronger.

To some people, Bitcoin still sounds like a crazy idea. But those who have embraced it can understand that at first it looked confusing but they are reaping the rewards now, and more is still to come. They say our greatest enemy is our fears, so let go of your fears, embrace it now, tell your family and friends, and encourage them to be part of the world's first decentralized digital currency. Who knows, you might just be the next Bitcoin millionaire.

More Books By George Icahn

Check out my Author Central Page:

http://www.cryptocurrencystudio.com/georgeicahn

www.ingramcontent.com/pod-product-compliance
Lightning Source LLC
Chambersburg PA
CBHW071156240526
45470CB00016BA/77